INSIGHT GUIDES

SHANGHAI
smart guide

APA PUBLICATIONS L

Part of the Langenscheidt Publishing Group

Contents

Highlights

▲ **Pudong** A fast-rising financial centre dominated by new skyscrapers and some of the world's most innovative architecture.
▶ **Shanghai Museum** Chinese art and artefacts presented in user-friendly fashion.

▲ **Xintiandi** A faux lane-house neighbourhood bristling with high-end shops, restaurants and nightclubs.

◀ **The Bund** With stately buildings on one side and the Huangpu River on the other, the Bund is one of the world's must-see sights.

▲ **Former French Concession** Loved for its leafy streets, fine architecture, and dazzling selection of cafes, pubs and boutiques.
◀ **Yuyuan** A Ming-era historic site surrounded by teeming lanes full of street vendors.

Shanghai

Bold in vision and rich in opportunity, Shanghai is a place where dreams are realised. It is a grand and ambitious city, filled with high-tech toys and home to some of the world's finest hotels and restaurants. It is also a city with a past, a place of classy old buildings and time-honoured temples and traditional lifestyles. From former fame to future glory there is not a more evocative city on earth.

Shanghai Fact and Figures

Population in 2010: **19 million**
Population in 1990: **13 million**
Migrant population: **7 million**
Area: **6,218 sq km (2,400 sq miles)**
Average January temperature: **4°C (39°F)**
Average July temperature: **30°C (86°F)**
Hottest recorded temperature: **41°C (106°F)**
Wettest month: **June**
Number of Metro lines in 2005: **2**
Number of Metro lines in 2010: **12**
Price of a 3km (2-mile) taxi ride: **rmb12, or US$1.75**

The City Moderne

Shanghai may well be the world's most dynamic city. After pausing for four decades, the city roared into life in the 1980s, as roads, bridges and buildings sprang from the flat sand, and money and people poured in, generating a high-voltage buzz that now resonates in every corner of the globe. The sheer energy of Shanghai attracts visitors from all seven continents, and its dizzying array of shopping, dining, sightseeing and partying possibilities keeps them endlessly entertained.

Shanghai is a city of sharply defined neighbourhoods. The Bund was always unique, and the other early settlements, Old Town and the foreign concessions, both had walls and were self-governed, so they developed their own street layouts and building styles. These boundaries remain obvious, and often the simple act of crossing a street is like entering another country or another era. After browsing among the skyscrapers and luxury malls of Nanjing West Road, a shopper might turn a corner and find a quiet café in a tree-lined old French Concession lane, or a pedestrian might exit a classical building on the Bund and immediately enter the rich and atmospheric lanes of Old Town.

Shanghai is also divided by geography. Looping, circuitous Suzhou Creek creates a north–south barrier, while the frenetic Huangpu River divides the city into east and west. Each of these semi-isolated areas has also developed a distinct character. Hongkou

Above: Duolun Road.

offers a mix of concession-era buildings, Chinese lane-house neighbourhoods and modern high-rises, while Western Shanghai has a similar mix of styles, but with bigger parks and roomier shopping malls. As always, Pudong is a world unto itself, a fast-rising boomtown of brand-new buildings that is still a work in progress.

Melting Pot

Shanghai is a city of opportunity, a money-rich magnet that attracts immigrants from all over China, who work on its construction sites, in its homes and restaurants and in the factories that ring the suburbs. Many have settled in Shanghai, and their regional dialects, strong country accents and authentic cuisines add to the city's appeal. They are joined by the Shanghainese, the colourful original residents whose brashness, business savvy and outspokenness remind many visitors of New Yorkers or Hong Kong Chinese. The Chinese residents of Shanghai are joined by a United Nations rainbow of foreigners, many of them Asian, who have come to pursue their dreams in the world's most meteoric city.

Left: the Bund Sightseeing Tunnel.

The Other Shanghai

With its famous skyscrapers, high-end shopping centres, luxury hotels and other glitzy trappings, Shanghai looks like a super-rich city. But in reality, it is far from rich. It remains an up-and-coming metropolis that has large pockets of penury, and places where lifestyles remain insulated from the 21st century. These neighbourhoods are filled with colourful sights, including street-side games of cards and mah-jong, teahouses, birdcages, sidewalk stands selling local specialities, mobile food carts and other features of local life.

Dining and drinking are Shanghai's most popular pastimes, with shopping a close second. The restaurant options are almost endless, and as for shopping, China's role as an epicentre of cheap manufacturing has spawned a huge cottage industry of street-side markets and sidewalk vendors, which exist side by side with designer boutiques and bespoke clothing stores and other pricey outlets.

Violent crime is rare in Shanghai, but pickpocketing and short-changing and petty theft are common, so secure your belongings.

The Bund

The imposing classical buildings of the Bund, lined up along the Huangpu River in an impressive row of pillars and stonework, are the most famous sight in Shanghai. Here, starting 100 years ago, British, Chinese, French and American merchants built a grand row of buildings that still typifies Shanghai's love of trade and commerce. Nestled in those iconic buildings are the classiest nightclubs, hotels and restaurants in town, many of them superbly designed to highlight their century-old surroundings, while behind the riverfront facade lies a neighbourhood of bookstores, cafés and commercial buildings that is ripe for exploration.

See Atlas page 140

0   200 m

0   200 yds

Bund Buildings

Customs House ①, with its signature clock tower and hourly chimes, and its next-door neighbour, the **Hongkong and Shanghai Bank Building** (now the Pudong Development Bank), with its precision stonework and dramatic dome, are the most famous classical buildings on the Bund. But the exclamation mark among the Bund buildings is the **Fairmont Peace Hotel** ②, an

elegant, eye-catching Art Deco period piece that is one of the most beautiful buildings in China.
SEE ALSO ARCHITECTURE, P.28, 29; ART DECO, P.34; HOTELS, P.68

Bund 18 and Three on the Bund

These two structures – the numbers refer to their addresses – are the Bund's most successful makeovers. **Bund 18**, home to **Bar Rouge** and **Lounge 18** nightclubs, **Mr and Mrs Bund Restaurant**, and a handful of fancy boutiques and coffee shops, is an authentic renovation that retains many original fea-

tures, and is highly regarded by architects and historians. **Three on the Bund**, home to **Laris**, **Jean Georges** and **New Heights** restaurants, a giant **Armani** shop, the **Shanghai Gallery of Art** and other attractions, is a

It is not your imagination: some of the Bund buildings are lean-ing, particularly the Yangtze Insurance Building at No. 26, which is tilted southwards at a sharp angle. The heavy build-ings are slowly sinking into the sandy mud of the Yangtze delta, and subsidence remains a serious problem in Shanghai, even for modern architects.

Left: Nanjing East
Pedestrian Road.

and the area features hotels and restaurants with Bund-style ambience, but without the high prices. Eventually the classical stone structures give way to a mixed commercial and residential neighbourhood that fewer tourists visit, despite its reasonably priced shops and restaurants. With a central location, this is a neighbourhood in flux, with new office towers and nightclubs rising from the flat residential blocks, along with a handful of hotel renovations and a couple of new malls, scattered among lanes and streets that remain local in character. Shanghai's **Foreign Languages Bookstore** ⑤ lies in this maze of blocks, as well as some of its best nightclubs, while **Fuzhou Road**, running from the Bund to People's Park, is famous for its art supply and stationery stores.

SEE ALSO FILM AND LITERATURE, P.61; SHOPPING, P.117

Nanjing Road East ⑥

Nanjing East is a famous 2km (1 mile) thoroughfare that connects People's Park to the Bund waterfront. This busy pedestrian-only street is a Mecca for tourists from around the world, and accents and dialects from the four corners of China combine with the tongues of Europeans and North Americans. There is plenty of local shopping to be done here, but people-watching is the primary pastime, preferably from one of the many alfresco sidewalk cafés.

SEE ALSO SHOPPING, P.117

total makeover that replaced the original interiors with a dazzling modern design.

SEE ALSO ARCHITECTURE, P.29, 30; BARS AND CAFÉS, P.36; MUSEUMS AND GALLERIES, P.82; NIGHTLIFE, P.88, 90; RESTAURANTS, P.100, 101

The Waterfront

In the spring of 2010, the Bund waterfront reopened after an eight-month renovation that added a new **tunnel** ③ to hide the car traffic, a bigger and more user-friendly **waterfront park**, and a new **dock** ④ for boats offering **river cruises**. Boat trips up and down the Huangpu River remain one of the Bund's top attractions.

SEE ALSO WALKS AND VIEWS, P.128

Behind the Bund

The classical buildings of the Bund extend back from the waterfront for several blocks,

Above left: Bund 18.
Left: fashion show at Three on the Bund.

Old Town

Old Town was Shanghai's original settlement, and it remains the most authentic Chinese neighbourhood in the city. Its narrow, winding lanes and local homes are bursting with sights and sounds, and its atmosphere harks back to an older, more traditional China, where the modern world has made fewer inroads. It has a vibrant street life, from morning t'ai chi to boisterous midday games of chess, to street vendors who emerge at dusk with blazing woks and tasty snacks. Ming-era temples and gardens, souvenir-shopping, and the most famous teahouse in China are among its many attractions.

Cool Docks

To protect it from pirate raids, the original walled city (now the centre of Old Town) was built several blocks from the Huangpu River, and the area between Old Town and the river languished for decades. But no longer: **Cool Docks**, a glistening new restaurant and nightlife complex on the Old Town waterfront, has emerged as one of the fastest-growing dine-and-drink complexes in Shanghai, and its state-of-the-art bars, restaurants and coffee shops, waterfront location and nearness to Yuyuan Garden have proved very popular.

Yuyuan Shangchanag (Yu Garden Bazaar) ①

Yuyuan is a vast warren of traditional-style lanes and buildings wrapped around the

Ming-era Yu garden *(Yuyuan)* itself, and punctuated by the celebrated Mid-Lake Teahouse, with its sweeping eaves and landmark location. The bazaar is packed with

souvenir vendors selling every conceivable knick-knack from Mao trinkets to mah-jong sets to T-shirts to 'antique' posters of 1930s beauties, plus just about everything else you might imagine. Old though it is, Yuyuan has modern commercial touches, such as neon signs, Western and Chinese fast food, and multiple mass-produced goods.

This is also an area rife with teashops, selling the finest leaves from the four corners of China. The area is filled with the rich scent of oolong and green tea from

Left: South Bund Fabric Market.

Left and below: Yuyuan Garden.

lotus, osmanthus, plum and bamboo leaf in different seasons, providing year-round visual pleasure. A carefully balanced blend of plants, pagodas, water and rocks, often with graceful balconies that overlook the best views, Yuyuan is a peaceful retreat from the noisy city that surrounds it.

SEE ALSO BARS AND CAFÉS, P.36; PARKS AND GARDENS, P.99

Shouning Road ④

Adventurous eaters and sightseers will find this local strip of indoor-outdoor eateries to be a treasure trove of local treats, all of them fresh and all of them very affordable. Among the tastiest snacks are *you bing*, a rich, flat, savoury pastry, fried crayfish and steamed dumplings. The blocks around Shouning Road provide a doorway into a more traditional era, when people had more time to gather and socialise. In the evenings, the streets come to life, as residents emerge to play with their kids, practise ballroom dancing, drink tea and chat with one another and with foreign visitors too, if they can speak even a little Chinese.

City God temples are the most active temples in any given town, and so it is with Shanghai's **Cheng Huang** (City God) shrine, a rambunctious place where worshippers throw oracle bones, burn incense and candles, and offer paper money to please their Taoist gods. *See also Churches and Temples, p.46*

ing Chashe) offers a welcome contrast to the buy-and-sell fervour of the bazaar, and the same applies to the cosy confines of **Yuyuan Garden** itself. The Ming-era garden is rendered in classic Jiangnan (south of the Yangtze) style, with moon bridges, jagged 'west lake' rockery, four-season garden layouts with flowers and plants that bloom or leaf throughout the year:

nearby Hangzhou, or heartier black pu'er tea from Yunnan, and interested tea buyers can sit down and taste a few cups before they buy. Also nearby are **Shiliu Puhong Qixiang Cloth Market** ② and **South Bund Fabric Market** ③, which have the lowest-cost tailoring and the broadest selection of fabrics in town.

SEE ALSO SHOPPING, P.116

Yuyuan Garden

With its calm, quiet rooms and aromatic pots of tea, the **Mid-Lake Teahouse** (Huxint-

9

People's Park Area

People's Park is an oasis and a refuge, a welcome patch of green space filled with fountains, lotus ponds and shady pathways which is encircled by tall buildings and embraced by the non-stop energy of Shanghai. The large oval park is a cultural hub, with four fine museums and a beautiful performance centre, and it has a handful of unique restaurants and lounges. It sits smack in the middle of town, surrounded by five-star hotel towers, classic Art Deco buildings, historic churches and mixed residential areas, forming a representative slice of the city itself.

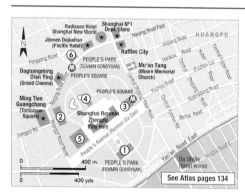

The Shanghai Art Museum was once the **Shanghai Race Club**, which overlooked the horse-racing track itself. The museum's finely crafted interiors retain a number of racing details, including betting windows on the ground floor and brass horse-head designs on the banisters and railings.

broad, flat topography.
SEE ALSO PARKS AND GARDENS, P.99

Inside the Park

People's Park is divided by a busy road into two halves – a park and a square – and the two halves are quite different in character. The southern half is a shady, tree-filled haven with winding garden paths, lotus ponds and a handful of bars and restaurants, while the northern half, or **People's Square**, is a Chinese-style plaza with broad empty patches of pavement, a couple of government buildings and plenty of open space. The entire area was once a horse-racing track, which is evident in its oval shape and

Museums of People's Park

The finest museums in the city are clustered inside the borders of People's Park. **Shanghai Museum** ① boasts a wonderful collection of Chinese art that is housed in a comfortable new building and accompanied by explanations in several languages.

Shanghai Art Museum ② hosts top global art exhibitions, including the Shanghai Biennale, and has a fine collection of modern Asian art, while the **Shanghai Urban Planning and Exhibition Centre** ③, with its dramatic dioramas of the Shanghai cityscape, also attracts

Left: Shanghai Art Museum. **Right:** Shanghai Grand Theatre.

Left: People's Park.

glass facade of **Raffles City** mall and the spaghetti-strand layers of the east–west expressway.

The park does not lack refreshing venues from which to view this parade of buildings; both the Museum of Contemporary Art and the Shanghai Art Museum have rooftop restaurants, while the skyline can also be glimpsed from **Barbarossa Lounge**.
SEE ALSO ARCHITECTURE, P.31,32; ART DECO, P.35; BARS AND CAFÉS, P.36; CHURCHES AND TEMPLES, P.46; HOTELS, P.70; SHOPPING, P.113, 117

Beyond the Park

Because of its city-centre location, each of the areas around People's Park contains a representative slice of cityscape. To the east is the Bund and to the south is Xintiandi, while to the north are the familiar tree-lined streets, high-end shopping and well-located hotels that highlight the nearby **Nanjing Road West** area. City government buildings dominate the neighbourhood to the west, but a careful search will uncover some nuggets, including inexpensive noodle and dumpling restaurants, and the wonderful Art Deco-style **Grand Cinema**.
SEE ALSO ART DECO, P.34

enthusiastic crowds. Those three are joined by the pocket-sized **Museum of Contemporary Art (MoCA)** ④, a former greenhouse that specialises in whacky displays of modern art. The park's final cultural highlight is **Shanghai Grand Theatre** ⑤, which hosts Broadway musicals and other lavish stage shows, along with more intimate performances in its two smaller theatres.
SEE ALSO MUSEUMS AND GALLERIES, P.82, 83; MUSIC, P.87

Near the Park

People's Park is fronted on all sides by a visual feast of architecture that includes the ultra-modern **Tomorrow Square** and **Shimao Towers**, the red-brick **Moore Memorial Church**, the **Radisson Hotel** with its 'flying saucer' crown, the soaring, Art Deco-style **Park Hotel** ⑥ and its equally venerable neighbour the **Pacific Hotel**, the stately brick **Shanghai Number One Department Store**, and the

Xintiandi Area

In 2002, an old lane-house district was converted into Xintiandi, a pedestrian-friendly combination of open-air mall, public plaza and street fair that is a must-see for most tourists. Xintiandi bristles with high-end restaurants, coffee shops, nightclubs and fancy boutiques, some of them excellent, and all of them upscale. Restaurants here fall into two categories: tried-and-true venues that are Shanghai institutions, and cutting-edge fusion restaurants that try to one-up each other in radical cuisine and fancy decor. For visitors, it's a win-win situation.

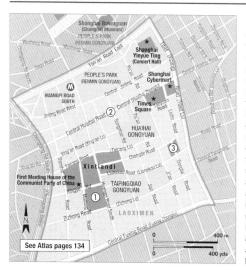

See Atlas pages 134

The main walking thoroughfare slices from through the middle of the development from north to south, and a large collection of restaurants and clubs can be found on this strip. But the area along **Huangpi Road**, a narrow maze of close-set walls and tiny pathways, is also worth exploring, and a walk through here will yield smaller, out-of-the-way bars and restaurants, along with a couple of historical sites, including the site of the first meeting of the Communist Party of China, which is now a small museum with free admission (House 15, North Block, Xintiandi).

Xintiandi

Xintiandi is not an authentic renovation, and many of the original *shikumen* (stone gate) homes were moved or rebuilt to make the area more retail-friendly. There is a rebuilt *shikumen* house in Xintiandi that is open to visitors, and it provides an insightful look at life in a lane house, but if you wish to see the real thing, genuine *shikumen* neighbourhoods can still be found, especially within the borders of the old French Concession.

The layout of Xintiandi (the name means 'new paradise') is not quite as simple as it looks.

Southern Xintiandi

At its southern end, Xintiandi's lane-house layout morphs into the **South Block**

Left: lunch at Crystal Jade in Xintiandi *(see p.102)*.

China. And at the east end of the street, where Huaihai Road meets Xizang Road, lies the new **Shanghai Cybermart**, a brightly lit warren of electronics vendors that offers rock-bottom prices on every computer-related item imaginable.
SEE ALSO SHOPPING, P.114, 115

Dongtai Road Antiques Market ③

The tables and stalls of these streetside vendors groan with modern gimcracks like Mao heads, tea sets, stone lions and Little Red Books. But the real gems of Dongtai Road are found in the surrounding lanes and alleys, where out-of-the-way shops restore and sell genuine Art Deco-era antique lamps and furniture. For serious antique collectors, Dongtai Road is a must-visit.
SEE ALSO SHOPPING, P.112

> The success of Xintiandi has spawned a host of competitors, and most cities in China now have at least one 'Xintiandi' of their own, and some, like Suzhou, have several.

Plaza ①, and this is its least visited and least popular section. The developers were not convinced the lane-house-style renovation would work and wanted to hedge their bets, so they insisted that this part of Xintiandi would be made into a shopping mall. Like the rest of Xintiandi, it contains some classy restaurants, but they are surrounded by a very ordinary selection of air-conditioned retail outlets.

Around Xintiandi

The area around Xintiandi contains the city's most sought-after residential addresses, where rows of cranes are busy building the priciest condos in town, along with some expensive hotels. Beneath the construction is a booming retail zone that is bursting with restaurants of all kinds, from classy Japanese noodles to convivial Chinese dumplings to Western diner food, along with a heady trawl of boutiques, banks, department stores and booksellers, plus a couple of small but pleasant parks.

Huaihai Road Central ②

The area's signature street is Huaihai Road, a target-rich stretch of retail that is anchored by **Times Square**, a shiny six-storey emporium that features the ever-popular **Zara**, famous for its trendy but wallet-friendly fashions, and **Chaterhouse Booktrader**, which has a fine selection of books about

Left: Xintiandi skyline.
Right: Dongtai Road Market.

13

Hongkou and Suzhou Creek

Hongkou is a quilted patchwork of diverse neighbourhoods, where luxury hotel towers and beautiful old buildings sit side by side with traditional residential quarters that seldom see tourists. The Suzhou Creek waterfront was once a warehouse district but has undergone a renaissance and is now lightly dotted with modern art galleries, sophisticated restaurants and classic buildings, while further inland, it becomes a residential area and commercial zone where a small but growing number of cutting-edge clubs and galleries have sprung up to catch Hongkou's overspill.

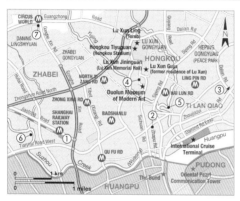

Transport Hub

Shanghai's new subways, especially Line 3 and Line 8, have pulled Hongkou closer to downtown Shanghai, making attractions like Duolun Road, ERA Intersection of Time circus and 1933 Old Millfun more accessible, while the core of Hongkou, which includes the new international cruise area, lies just across Suzhou Creek from the Bund, and is becoming a prime tourist zone.

Hongkou also features **Shanghai Railway Station** ①, while further afield are **Zhapu Road** ② food street, a cosy collection of restaurants and street stalls, and the enormous **Gongqing Forest Park** ③, a fun-filled attraction that takes an entire day to see.

SEE ALSO PARKS AND GARDENS, P.98

International Cruise Area

The giant new **Shanghai Port International Cruise** Terminal can berth three 300m (984ft) cruise ships at one time, and a growing number of global cruise lines have put Shanghai on their itineraries. The surrounding area, which is just a few minutes from the Bund, is benefiting from the explosion in foot traffic, and has sprouted a collection of hotels, restaurants and retail outlets.

SEE ALSO TRANSPORT, P.122

Duolun Road ④

This kilometre-long (½-mile) semi-pedestrian strip is dotted with bronze statues of the Chinese writers and filmmakers who lived in Shanghai 100 years ago. The most famous is **Lu Xun**, and he is joined in bronze by Guo

scratching (heaps of metal, globs of plastic) to beautifully rendered painting and sculpture, with everything in between.
SEE ALSO MUSEUMS AND GALLERIES, P.83, 84

Circus World ⑦

The **ERA Intersection of Time** circus is fast-paced and professional, and its performers are selected from the finest acrobatics schools in China. The well-choreographed show involves dozens of breathtaking – and sometimes death-defying – acts of balance, magic and acrobatics, to the accompaniment of live music. Its most famous act is an edge-of-the-seat thriller in which half a dozen motorcyclists speed around the inside of a giant glass globe (Shanghai Circus World, 2266 Gonghexin Road; tel: 6652 7750; www.era-shanghai.com; daily 7.30pm; admission; Metro: Line 1, Circus World).

Lu Xun is Shanghai's most famous literary figure, and his mausoleum is in Lu Xun Park, also in Hongkou. His best-known book, *The True Story of Ah Q*, is a wonderful story about a man who easily explains away all the bad things that happen to him.

Moruo, Ding Ling and many others, along with a surprise statue of Charlie Chaplin, who visited Shanghai in 1931. Statues aside, the street's highlights are the **Old Film Café**, the **Osage** art gallery, and the **Duolun Museum of Modern Art**.
SEE ALSO FILM AND LITERATURE, P.60; WALKS AND VIEWS, P.129

1933 Old Millfun/ The Factory ⑤

This former slaughterhouse is another eye-catching Shanghai makeover, a vast maze of interlocking ramps, staircases and suspended bridges that was carefully renovated, staying true to the original but sparkling with modern glass and steel fittings. Cafés, bakeries, art galleries and shops have moved in, making it a tourist attraction, and so have art, fashion and design firms, turning it into a 'creative cluster' like Taikang Road, except with cheaper rents.

50 Moganshan Road ⑥

This area is an art lover's dream, a collection of lanes and warehouses that is chock-a-block with galleries of all sizes, from small boutiques to warehouse-sized spaces that feature giant sculptures and wall-to-ceiling paintings. **M50** had modest beginnings, as a few galleries began to promote local artists, but with the rapid growth in global interest in modern Chinese art, the neighbourhood boomed. The artworks range from head-

15

Nanjing Road West Area

With its high-end malls, luxury outlets and soaring office towers, Nanjing Road West is the modern face of Shanghai. Nestled beneath the towers are the most stylish shoppers and best-dressed office workers in town. They are joined by bag-toting tourists in search of the latest fashions. But the luxury veneer is thin, and just off Nanjing Road are those Shanghai staples: lane-house neighbourhoods bursting with local life, and tree-lined streets filled with mixed – though still upscale – residential neighbourhoods that are sprinkled with fun little cafés, nightclubs, boutique hotels and other attractions.

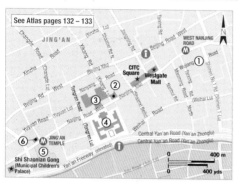

See Atlas pages 132 – 133

Wujiang Pedestrian Street ①

This recent development is another Shanghai success story, a former backstreet and parking lot that was converted in 2007, with very little fuss, into an energetic four-block, pedestrian-only strip lined with affordable alfresco cafés, coffee and ice-cream shops, sit-down Chinese restaurants and shops. Just a block from Nanjing Road itself, it presents an entirely different shopping and dining experience that is quieter and more local in character.

Shopping Malls

The soaring **Plaza 66** ② tower, with the landmark 'light box' at its apex, and its sister-in-luxury, **Citic Square**, are the two most exclusive malls in town. The haute couture is relieved by a bookstore or two and a clutch of classy, white-tablecloth restaurants, but you won't find a food court at either of these highbrow addresses. A block or two down the street to the east, and a rung or two down the luxury ladder, is the ever-popular **Westgate Mall**. The department stores and shops and restaurants of Westgate are always busy, a testament to Shanghai's love of a bargain, while the mall's central atrium offers fashion shows filled with leggy models, stage shows demonstrating different products, and other action-packed entertainments.
SEE ALSO SHOPPING, P.113, 114

Shanghai Centre ③

Although it only opened in 1990, **Shanghai Centre** is a venerable address, loved by residents for its convenience, by architects for its unique design, and by visitors for its bars, restaurants and stage shows. Designed to look like the Chinese character shan, or mountain, the three towers

Left: Shanghai Exhibition Centre.

every night with live bands, pool tables, dancing, bar games, tequila shots and other boozy activities that attract fun-loving drinkers from Shanghai and around the world. Scattered among the bars are a few late-night eateries, but it is rumoured that the area will be closed for Expo 2010.

Jing'an Park and Temple

The goldfish ponds, jagged 'west lake' rockery, children's play area and towering Eurasian plane trees of **Jing'an Park** ⑤ make it a rare neighbourhood oasis, filled with early-morning t'ai chi and the mid-afternoon shouts of playful children, while **Jing'an Temple** ⑥ is a landmark cherry-red Buddhist shrine that features a Ming-era copper bell and some notable stone Buddhas, among other antiquities. Like most temples in China, it is more popular as a tourist attraction than as a place of worship.
SEE ALSO CHURCHES AND TEMPLES, P.47

Because **luxury taxes** raise the price of high-end goods in Shanghai by more than 30%, many residents prefer to buy their watches, jewellery and designer clothes in Hong Kong or Macau.

of Shanghai Centre contain a hotel, serviced apartments and offices, and beneath the towers is a welcoming warren of concrete and rockery, beset by the beckoning neon glow of the shops on its perimeters, and highlighted by the feng shui-friendly waterfall that trickles down the central tower of the **Portman Ritz-Carlton** hotel. Across from the centre is one of the most visible landmarks in town, the **Shanghai Exhibition Centre** ④. Built by the Soviet Union in the mid-1950s, and capped by a

glowing red star, the old exhibition centre continues to host many of the city's most popular exhibitions.
SEE ALSO ARCHITECTURE, P.31, 32; HOTELS, P.72

Tongren Road

This sparkling galaxy of beerhouses and nightclubs hums

Left: Plaza 66. **Right:** Jing'an Temple.

Former French Concession North

The beloved old French Concession is a quintessential slice of Shanghai. Around every corner lies a gem of some sort: a freshly renovated century-old villa, a charming alfresco café, a cosy, pocket-sized pub or a half-forgotten historical relic with a dusty plaque and a sleepy attendant. Few of Shanghai's must-see sights are here – its enduring appeal lies instead in its quiet charm, subtle delights and rich, compact density.

The Value of Preservation

While the original borders of the old French Concession have long since disappeared, its outline is still apparent, and the contrast with the rest of Shanghai is remarkable.

Much of the old concession is still low-rise, and it is filled with lane-houses and old apartments; it has more green space than the rest of Shanghai, although sometimes the grass and trees lie behind walls and in villa compounds that require some dedicated exploration to reach.

Much of the old concession is administered by the Xuhui district government, which has earned a reputation for preservation, and stresses careful development, rather than the wholesale rebuilding that typifies the rest of Shanghai.

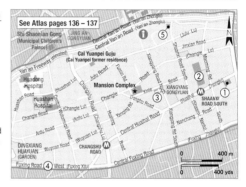

Changle, Xinle and Shaanxi Roads

This trio of interconnected streets is ideal for a casual exploration on foot or by bicycle. Shoppers will find a treasure trove of small local boutiques that offer rare bargains on brand-name fashions, shelves filled with local designs, and factory seconds that can be had for a very low price. The boutiques share the leafy streets with a generous selection of restaurants, bookstores, coffee shops and teahouses.

Of the three roads, Shaanxi Road has more clothing stores, while the others have a few more dine-and-drink venues, especially Western restaurants. Towering over the low-rise streets are two well-known hotels, the Art Deco-style **Jinjiang** ①, and the high-rise **Okura Garden** ②, with its acres of parkland.
SEE ALSO FASHION, P.58, 59; HOTELS, P.74

> The vast shady canopies and jigsaw-puzzle bark of the ever-present **Eurasian plane trees** are a defining feature of the old concession. A cross between an American Sycamore and an Asian Plane, the stately trees grow profusely during the humid Shanghai summers, despite receiving a very drastic pruning each winter.

Donghu Road

This charming two-block strip of tree-lined street has quickly become one of the top dining areas in the city. The array of restaurants offers everything a hungry visitor might ask for, including Japanese, Mexican, Italian, Cantonese, American and more, and the street includes a broad selection of price points, from the city's

Left: shopping for lucky charms on Xinle Road.

spires of the recently renovated **Russian Orthodox Mission Church** ③.

Fuxing Road West ④

If you're going to walk just once in Shanghai, make it Fuxing West Road. This tree-lined street, with its classic pre-war architecture, intimate lane-house neighbour- hoods and generally low-rise buildings, is a fine place to soak up the concession atmosphere. It also boasts a fine selection of architecture, from Art Deco and Moderne townhouses to English Tudor-style mansions, to California-inspired Moorish revival homes. Nor is it lacking in refreshment: Fuxing West features a bright galaxy of eateries and watering holes that includes a designer brewpub, an intimate Yunnanese restaurant, a pair of jazz clubs and a selection of coffee shops and bakeries.

most expensive sushi to quick and easy cafés selling hamburgers and noodles. The exclamation mark on Donghu Road is the **Mansion complex**, a new development that opened in 2008 with a lively collection of 10 or 12 restaurants and nightclubs that share the same broad alfresco patio. A short walk west down equally lively Xinle Road is another neighbourhood landmark: the bright-blue onion-dome

The gingerbread spires and fantasy castle turrets and profound playfulness of **Hengshan Moller Villa** ⑤ *(right)* have turned it into a favourite local landmark. Built in 1938 by Swedish shipping magnate Eric Moller, it is now a small hotel, where visitors can admire the delightful East-West hotchpotch of gold-painted furniture, parquet wood floors, marble pillars, wood panelling, spiral staircases, leaded glass windows and other extravagant design elements. *See also Architecture, p.30, 31; Hotels, p.73.*

Former French Concession South

The southern half of the old concession has the same hole-in-the-wall vendors, teashops and cafés that spill onto the sidewalks, boutique stores, period architecture, tree-lined streets and appealing atmosphere as the northern section. The south is more raucous – the bigger, boozier nightclubs are here, and the livelier neon-lit bar strips. But the approach is the same: follow your heart down any lane or street, and you can't possibly go wrong.

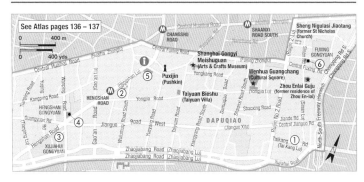

Taikang Lu ①

Taikang Lu, or Tian Zi Fang, is a popular enclave filled with shops and galleries that offer a variety of jewellery, crafts, pottery, paintings, books, local designer clothes and so on, refreshed by a selection of semi-bohemian cafés and restaurants and teashops. Unlike Xintiandi, which is largely recreated, Taikang Lu grew naturally, and it still features its original *shikumen* (stone gate) homes, concession-era apartments and warehouse space, although decorated with a touch of modern Shanghai.
SEE ALSO FASHION, P.59; SHOPPING, P.117

Right: outdoor art on Taikang Lu.

Hengshan Road

Hengshan Road is the liveliest strip in the neighbourhood, and an evening stroll down its 1km (½-mile) length will yield a wealth of night-time options, from cheerful English pubs to lavishly redesigned villas that

have plenty of courtyard space and ultra-popular ladies' nights, to local bars with neon signs, sidewalk seating, dim interiors and low prices. If the cocktails and canapés don't fill you up – or the beer and peanuts, as the

Left: ballroom dancing takes to Fuxing Park.

Russian Poet Alexander Pushkin, is the epicentre of another charming area. Dozens of dine-and-drink options beckon from within a block or two, alongside a century-old mansion that is now the **Shanghai Museum of Arts and Crafts**, and the famous **Shanghai Conservatory of Music** ⑤, which offers student concerts at reasonable prices.
SEE ALSO MUSEUMS AND GALLERIES, P.85; MUSIC, P.86

Fuxing Park

In general, the old concession is not rich in standard tourist sights, because most of the city's early history occurred on the Bund and in Old Town, and most of the new attractions were built in Pudong and People's Park. But the Fuxing Park area is an exception. It boasts the **former residences of Sun Yat-sen** ⑥ and **Zhou En-lai**, an old Russian church, and tall, glowering, side-by-side statues of Karl Marx and Friedrich Engels, staring boldly into a future that no longer exists. History aside, the park is a cheerful collection of grass and trees where the Shanghai-ren relax and play.
SEE ALSO PARKS AND GARDENS, P.98

case may be – there are restaurants galore, including a lively late-night dining strip on Hengshan Road just west of Wulumuqi Road, across from the Shanghai Community Church, also called the **International Church** ②. At the southern end of Hengshan is **Xujiahui Park** ③, a landscaped oasis filled with ponds, skating paths, trees and playgrounds. The park's

northern corner is dominated by the huge yellow facade of the historic **Hengshan Picardie Hotel** ④, while across the street lies the tiny, tree-lined retreat of Hengshan Park.
SEE ALSO CHURCHES AND TEMPLEST, P.47; HOTELS, P.75

The Pushkin Triangle

This tiny triangular park, highlighted by a bust of the

Even in Shanghai's quietest neighbourhood, the streets and sidewalks are often packed with people. The population pressure in China's biggest city is enormous, and more people move in every day – at the end of 2008, Shanghai had 19 million people, up from 16 million in 2000 and 13 million in 1990.

Western Shanghai

Western Shanghai starts with a bang in Xujiahui, a pulsating hub of high-rise shopping malls, apartment blocks and historical sights on the edge of the old French Concession, and it ends with a whimper in the factory- and farm-filled flatlands of the distant Yangtze delta. In between are some low-key but fun attractions, including a zoo, several parks, a thousand-year-old temple and a pedestrian-only bar-and-restaurant strip, plus one very high-voltage venue, the Formula One racetrack. Many overseas Chinese and other expats live here, attracted by the cheap rents, spacious parks and easy access to downtown and to the domestic airport.

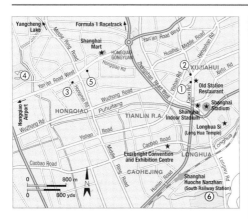

Above: Xujiahui Catholic Church.

Xujiahui

On the fringes of the old concession, and free from its low-rise building constraints, the city explodes into a high-rise hub of towering multi-storey shopping malls, warehouse stores, eateries of all kinds, and apartment and hotel and office blocks, all of them humming with humanity.

Xujiahui district has historical sights, notably **Xujiahui Catholic Church** ①, **Old Station restaurant** and **Long Hua Temple**, but much of it, including **Grand Gateway Mall** ②, **Shanghai Stadium** and **Shanghai Indoor Stadium**, is brand new. Because it targets the middle class, the area offers abun-

dant hotel and retail bargains, and its low prices and city-centre location make it popular with both tourists and residents.

SEE ALSO CHURCHES AND TEMPLES, P.47; RESTAURANTS, P.110; SHOPPING, P.113

Hongmei Pedestrian Street ③

This cheerful strip of pubs, bakeries and ethnic restaurants sits in the middle of a bland suburb, but its food offerings draw the crowds not just from the surrounding areas, but from downtown Shanghai as well. The choices range from Korean barbecue to American burger baskets to expertly

hand-rolled Japanese sushi, while post-prandial options are equally plentiful, with dessert stands, coffee shops and comfortable barstools beckoning from every block.

Gubei and Hongqiao

These far western zones feature a suburban swirl of super stores, residential compounds, local shopping streets, school campuses, office buildings and the like, all connected by vast clusters

22

Left and below: Shanghai Botanical Garden.

nearing completion in the western suburbs. Its nine new towns are based on European patterns and are designed by top-flight foreign architects, and they are one-of-a-kind developments filled with eclectic homes. The German town of **Anting** was designed by German architect Albert Speer, with bent streets, tiny courtyards, medieval plazas and village-square fountains, and with room for 50,000 residents, while **Thames Town** includes pubs, a town square and a village-style church. The nearest one to Shanghai is **Pujiang Italian town**, while the biggest is **Linggang Harbour City**, a modern Chinese-style development that will house up to 800,000 residents. Dutch, Spanish, American and traditional Chinese towns round out the offerings.

Yangcheng Lake, in the far western suburbs, is home to the best-tasting hairy crabs in the world. During the October to December crab season, diners flock from Shanghai to the shores of the lake to feast on this rare delicacy. *See also Food and Drink, p.64*

The business attractions, along with the ongoing expansion of the Hongqiao domestic airport and the area's position as a crossroads between Shanghai, Nanjing and Hangzhou, ensure that Gubei and Hongqiao will remain vibrant for decades to come.

SEE ALSO ARCHITECTURE, P.31, 32; CHILDREN, P.45; PARKS AND GARDENS, P.99; SPORTS, P.121

One City Nine Towns

The ambitious One City Nine Towns satellite city plan is

of highway. In their midst are some notable tourist attractions, including **Shanghai Zoo** ④, **Hongqiao International Pearl Mall** ⑤, the **Formula One Racetrack**, **Shanghai Botanical Garden** ⑥ and, especially if you love modern architecture, the remarkable **Shanghai South Railway Station**.

The area is also rich in budget accommodation, and is home to some key business-related venues, such as **Shanghai Mart**, **Shanghai International Trade Centre**, and the **Everbright Convention and Exhibition Centre**.

Pudong

The heart of Pudong lies beneath the fast-growing forest of skyscrapers that sightseers love to look at from the Bund. Called Lujiazui, the area features museums, a popular mall, three towers with sky-high observation decks, and a riverfront park that is dotted with dining and drinking options. The ambitious World Expo 2010 site lies just to the south, while to the east are Shanghai's biggest park, its newest museum and its finest concert hall. Still further east, Pudong encompasses the Maglev train, the international airport, and a new exhibition hall, before fading into a seldom-visited expanse of farms, factories and residential blocks.

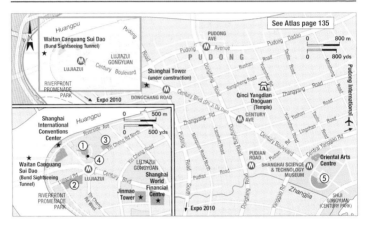

East of the River

Pudong means east of the Huangpu River, while Puxi, or Shanghai proper, means west of the river, and the east–west divide is razor sharp. On one side is Shanghai, with its iconic name, gripping history, lovely old architecture and crowded but atmospheric streets, while on the other is Pudong, with its broad boulevards, modern skyscrapers, abundant space and fast-rising financial centre.

A sharp rivalry exists between the two. Pudong residents praise their spacious parks, cheap rents, modern museums and concert venues, while Puxi residents deri-sively call their rival Pu-Jersey, and consider it merely an obstacle on their way to the airport. Despite the criticism, Pudong serves a useful purpose: it relieves the residential density of a city of nearly 20 million people.

Left: Century Park.

Tower – and each of them offers eagle-eye views of the great sprawling city of Shanghai. Further out is the most impressive **Shanghai Science and Technology Museum** ⑤

SEE ALSO ARCHITECTURE, P.33, MUSEUMS AND GALLERIES, P.85

The Hinterland

Beyond the waterfront and the financial district the bank towers and five-star hotels begin to fade away, to be replaced by factory-filled flatlands and endless blocks of buildings. The 522 sq km (200 sq mile) **Pudong New Area** lies on a vast expanse of land that contains a foreign trade zone, a financial zone, a high-tech zone, an export zone, a biotech zone, a tourist zone... you get the picture. But some of these zones are much visited by business travellers, and Pudong's outer ring of real estate has a number of affordable hotels and restaurants. The hinterland has infrastructure highlights as well, including the **Maglev train** that whizzes overhead at 430kmph (267mph), the ever-expanding **Pudong International Airport**, and **Jinqiao**, an upscale enclave of expat-centric shopping and dining.

SEE ALSO TRANSPORT, P.122

The Waterfront

The Huangpu River waterfront offers a rich menu of tourist attractions that includes the **Oriental Pearl Tower** ①, **Super Brand Mall** ②, **Shanghai Aquarium** ③, **Pudong Promenade Park**, **Bund Sightseeing Tunnel** and **Shanghai History Museum** ④, along with an only-in-Shanghai selection of cafés and restaurants. This is one of Shanghai's best walks, with views of the skyscrapers of Pudong on one side and the Bund on the other side, just across the river. Not far south of the promenade is **World Expo 2010**, a beyond-bold project that has transformed a former factory and dockyard district into a vast playground of Expo-related pavilions and buildings.

SEE ALSO ARCHITECTURE, P.32, 33; CHILDREN, P.44; EXPO 2010, P.54–5; MUSEUMS AND GALLERIES, P.85; SHOPPING, P.114; WALKS AND VIEWS, P.128, 129

The Financial District

Bristling with cranes and beset by construction sites, the financial district is home to many of the city's priciest office buildings, hotels and high-rises. China's tallest towers are here – the **Jinmao Tower** and the **Shanghai World Financial Centre**, which will soon be joined by the even loftier **Shanghai**

Left: Pudong's high-rise financial district. **Right:** the high-speed Maglev train.

A–Z

In the following section Shanghai's attractions and services are organised by theme, under alphabetical headings. Items that link to another theme are cross-referenced. All sights that are located within the atlas section at the end of the book are given a page number and grid reference.

Architecture

S hanghai architecture is a tale of two building booms. The first one, in the early to mid-1900s, gave the city its stately Bund buildings, its classy Art Deco period pieces, its unique Chinese-Western lane-house hybrids, and its whimsical, one-of-a-kind private villas. The second boom began in the 1990s and is ongoing, as an intoxicating mix of easy money and anything-goes high-rise architecture has fuelled the current fast-growing collection of glass-and-steel skyscrapers that is rapidly changing the city skyline. *See also Art Deco, p.34–5.*

Bund Beginnings

Old Shanghai architecture begins on the Bund, a long strip of stately structures that is the best-preserved collection of buildings in the city. These ponderous period pieces were built to impress visitors and embody the glory of the companies they housed, which were mostly in banking, insurance, trading and shipping. The 30 or so buildings, made mostly of imported materials, lie in a graceful arch near the Huangpu River, and with two eye-catching exceptions – the Fairmont Peace Hotel and the Old Bank of China – are pre-modern in style, with pillars, stonework and squat, sturdy classical designs.

The Bund has many exceptional buildings, and most are open to tourists – just walk in and have a look. One good example is the Yokohama Specie Bank, now the **ICBC Bank Building**; its dark doors open onto a spacious gilded lobby filled with eye-catching details. Next to Yokohama Bank is the Yangtze Insurance Building,

now the **Agricultural Bank of China**. One of the oldest buildings on the Bund, it leans south towards Yoko-hama Bank, and every year it leans a little more.

Two of the most remarkable Bund buildings sit side by side: **Customs House**, with its signature clock tower, and the Hongkong and Shanghai Bank Building, now the **Pudong Development Bank**. The Hongkong and Shanghai Bank Building was completed in 1923, by British architects Palmer and Turner, and their brief was an architect's dream: spare no

expense and dominate the Bund. This impressive structure is in the grand European style, with solid columns and archways topped by a vaulting dome.

The Hongkong Bank Building is a must-see; at night it glows like a jewel, and by day it showcases a domed lobby encircled by eight magnificent mosaics, depicting the financial capitals of the day.

Customs House
13 Zhongshan East No. 1 Road; tel: 6889 0000; Bus: 42, 910; map p.140 2B

Left: the stark interior of Bund 18.

Art Deco-Chinese hybrid with a curious pagoda-like top, which opened in 1937.

Two of the old buildings have been renovated for modern use, and are now among the top attractions on the Bund. The most authentic is **Bund 18**, a former bank building that reopened in 2004, and is now home to a restaurant, nightclub, and some classy boutiques and coffee shops. A walk through the stone columns and into the marbled lobby is like a trip back in time, and **Bar Rouge** itself is a gaudy late-night lounge that would not be amiss in the opium-saturated Shanghai of old. Another old-into-new renovation is **Three on the Bund**, which features a rebuilt interior, and houses an even more impressive collection of restaurants and boutiques.

In Hongkou, just north of the Bund, lie a couple more classics: **Waibaidu Bridge** and the **Pujiang Hotel**. Waibaidu Bridge, or the Iron-workers' Bridge, crosses Suzhou Creek and connects the Bund to Hongkou, as it has since 1907. The bridge reopened in 2008 following a top-to-bottom revamp that added glowing green, blue and purple neon lights, and polished the riveted girders

Shanghai's **lane-houses** are a unique East–West hybrid that exists nowhere else. The idea was copied from the terrace homes of London, but the homes are Chinese in style. Shanghai has two styles of lane house: the older *shikumen* (stone gate) homes have big gardens and wraparound courtyards with the signature stone gates. In the 1930s, as population increased, a new style of lane-house emerged, with narrower lanes and smaller, more vertical homes. A good example is Cite Bourgogne, on Shaanxi South Road just north of Jianguo Middle Road.

ICBC Bank Building, formerly the Yokohama Specie Bank
24 Zhongshan East No. 1 Road, on the Bund waterfront; map p.140 3B

Pudong Development Bank, formerly the

Above left: Hong Kong and Shanghai Bank Building.
Right: Astor House, now the Pujiang Hotel, *(see p.30)*.

Hongkong and Shanghai Bank Building
12 Zhongshan East No. 1 Road, on the Bund waterfront; tel: 6161 8888; Bus: 42, 910; map p.140 2B

A New Style

The Hongkong and Shanghai Bank Building marked the end of classical architecture in Shanghai, because in 1929 the Cathay Hotel opened, and that cutting-edge Art Deco tower, now the **Fairmont Peace Hotel**, announced the arrival of modern architecture in Shanghai.

Next to the Fairmont Peace Hotel is the **Old Bank of China Building**, a unique

and symmetrical iron-and-steel geometry into a high gloss.

A block away is the venerable Pujiang Hotel, formerly the Astor House, which is now a budget hotel, where walk-in visitors can stroll the teak-lined corridors and gaze at the high-ceilinged rooms. This was the top address in town when it reopened after a renovation in 1906, and its stone columns and arched porticoes evoke an era of steamship travel and exotic lifestyles; Charlie Chaplin and Albert Einstein both stayed there. The Pujiang is one of the two most authentic and unaltered old buildings in Shanghai; the other is the Hongkong and Shanghai Bank Building.
SEE ALSO NIGHTLIFE, P.88

Bund 18
18 Zhongshan East No. 1 Road, near Nanjing East Road on the Bund waterfront; tel: 6323 8099; www.bund18.com; Metro: Line 2, Nanjing East; Bus: 20; map p.140 B3

Fairmont Peace Hotel
20 Nanjing Road East, corner Nanjing Road and the Bund; tel: 10 800 714 1088; www.fairmont.com; Metro: Line 2, Nanjing East; Bus: 55, 910; map p.140 B3
SEE ALSO ART DECO, P.34; HOTELS, P.68

Pujiang Hotel, also called Astor House
15 Huangpu Road; tel: 6324 6388; www.pujianghotel.com; Metro: Line 2, Nanjing East, then 5-minute taxi; Bus: 868; map p.135 C4
SEE ALSO HOTELS, P.72

Private Endeavours
The banks and trading companies built their offices on the Bund, while away from the Bund were the foreign concessions, and these were the playgrounds of the tycoons, who threw up fanciful villas, stately compounds and extravagant clubhouses, in a variety of styles.

The most remarkable example is **Moller Villa**, built in 1938 by Swedish shipping magnate Eric Moller. The gingerbread spires, fantasy castle turrets and carefree playfulness of this remarkable rich man's fantasy are a singular local landmark. Wander in, have a drink at the bar and admire the swirling East–West mix of gold-painted furniture, parquet wood floors, marble pillars, wood panelling, spiral staircases, leaded stained-glass windows and other remarkable design features.

Another fine example of the extravagance of the ultra-rich is the **Children's Palace**, formerly the Marble Hall, which was completed in 1924 by the Kadoorie family. This huge family home is grand in every way, from the planta-

Many of Shanghai's lane-houses and some of its apartments face south, as dictated by **feng shui**, with the biggest windows and rooms facing south, and with tiny rooms for servants or students on the north. It is not uncommon, especially among the spider-web streets of the old French Concession, to see entire rows of lane-houses set at odd angles to the streets, so they can face south. A good example is the corner of Nanchang and Maoming South roads, in the old French Concession South.

tion-style lawn to the broad balcony to the interior halls. But its finest feature is the two-storey ballroom, a splendid hall of perfect size, with ornate columns and arched windows that soar upwards in perfect symmetry, before culminating in a curved ceiling that is rich in textured geometrical detail and subtly lit by glittering chandeliers.

Children's Palace, or Marble Hall

64 Yan'an West Road, near Huashan Road; tel: 6248 1850; www.cwkids.org; Bus: 71,48; map p.132 B1

Hengshan Moller Villa

30 Shaanxi Road South; tel: 6247 8881; www.moller villa.com; Metro: Line 2, Nanjing West, then taxi; Bus: 24; map p.133 D1
SEE ALSO HOTELS, P.73

Above: Shanghai Exhibition Centre. **Left:** Moller Villa's grand interior.

The Modern Era

From 1949 to 1990, few new buildings went up in Shanghai. One exception is the **Shanghai Exhibition Centre**, formerly the Sino-Soviet Friendship Hall, a unique period piece with amber-yellow exteriors and a Stalinist, wedding-cake central spire capped by a super-visible red star that glows brightly at night. Built by the Soviet Union in 1955 to illustrate the glories of Soviet Communism, it now hosts luxury marts that trumpet the virtues of capitalistic excess.

But the modern era really began with the **Shanghai Centre**, which opened in 1990 as the first large-scale multi-use building built in China since at least 1949. The three towers of the John Portman-designed complex recreate the Chinese character for mountain, while beneath, in a labyrinthine but effective layout, lies a superbly designed warren of bars, cafés, grocery

stores, acrobatic shows and other visitor-friendly amenities.

Another Nanjing Road beauty is the 285m (935ft) **Tomorrow Square**, a readily recognisable tower that features a 45° twist halfway up, where the building changes from serviced apartments into the **JW Marriott hotel**. Also on Nanjing Road, and almost as impressive, is the 288m (945ft) **Plaza 66**, a design best-known for the glowing 'light box' at its apex.

Not all of Shanghai's new buildings are for private use – the impressive **Shanghai South Railway Station**, which serves as the terminus for all southbound trains, is the world's only round railway

---

The word Bund, which was brought to Shanghai by the British, derives from the Indian word for embankment. It later came to mean a waterfront road, especially a waterfront road along an embankment.

Built on the sand and mud of the Yangtze River delta, Shanghai is sinking. As the groundwater was drained from beneath it, the city's support disappeared, and the weight of its buildings pushed it downwards. The problem peaked in the 1950s and 1960s, when the city sank nearly 4cm (1½in) per year. The government, alarmed at the prospect of a disappearing city, reduced the extraction of groundwater, and began pumping some of it back into the land. The subsidence has slowed to less than a centimetre per year, but with the annual addition of countless tonnes of steel and concrete, nobody is ready to declare victory.

Plaza 66
1266 Nanjing Road, by Shaanxi North Road; tel: 6279 0910; Metro: Line 2, between Jing'An and Nanjing West; Bus: 20, 24, 738; map p.133 C2

Shanghai Centre
1376 Nanjing Road West; tel: 6279 8600; Metro: Line 2, Jing'An; Bus: 37, 24, 921; map p.133 C2

Shanghai Exhibition Centre
1000 Yan'an Road; tel: 6279 0279; Metro: Line 2, Jing'An; Bus: 127, 71; map p.133 C1

Shanghai South Railway Station
8075 Humin Road, near Humin Expressway and Liuzhou Road; tel: 5436 9511; www.nzdq.org; Metro: Line 2, Shanghai South Railway

Tomorrow Square
399 Nanjing Road West, Puxi; Metro: Lines 1, 2, People's Square; map p.134 2A

Pudong

There are many other notable new structures in Puxi, but the epicentre of modern architecture is in Pudong, on the other

station, and it is a giant, at 278m (912ft) across and 48m (157ft) high. Shanghai South is a beauty to look at and a pleasure to use, with a dramatic skylit dome made of polycarbonate and aluminium and unsupported by pillars, which arches high above the passengers, and allows a welcome flood of daylight into the terminal.

side of the river, where the **Oriental Pearl Tower**, a 468m (1,535ft) tower that opened in 1994, marks the start of the modern era. With its unpainted concrete pillars and its futuristic hot-pink glass bubbles, to say nothing of its prime riverfront location, the Pearl Tower commands visual attention.

Nearby is the most beautiful and best-loved of the city's modern skyscrapers, the 421m (1,381ft) **Jinmao Tower**, which opened in 1998. A soaring, textured skyscraper topped by a Chinese-inspired pagoda-like roof, the Jinmao has multiple panes of glass that sparkle in the sun like the facets of a diamond. Another treat lies inside, where a dramatic central canyon creates a breathtaking interior space that is like nothing else on earth. Go to the Grand Hyatt lobby and have a look.

Next to the Jinmao is the 492m (1,614ft) **Shanghai World Financial Centre**, a dramatic grey-blue structure that rises from the flat soil of Pudong like a super-sized shark's fin. Viewed from the north and south, it has a broad base that displays a squat sturdiness, while from the Bund and elsewhere in downtown Shanghai it looks like a slender, elegant sail, with its trapezoid-shaped hole clearly visible at the roof-line. The World Financial Centre, which opened in 2008 and is home to the Park Hyatt Hotel, suffered from a late design change that replaced a planned circular top with a square one, giving it a new nickname – the bottle opener.

Jinmao Tower
88 Century Avenue, Pudong; tel: 5047 5101; Metro: Line 2, Lujiazui; Bus: 993; map p.135 E3

Oriental Pearl Tower
1 Century Avenue, Pudong; tel: 5879 8888; Metro: Line 2, Lujiazui; map p.135 4D

Shanghai World Financial Centre
100 Century Avenue, Pudong; tel: 6841 3000; tour centre tel: 6877 7878; www.swfc-shanghai.com; Metro: Line 2, Dong Chang Road; Bus: 1, 85, 584; map p.135 E3

Clockwise from left: Shanghai South Railway Station; Tomorrow Square; Jinmao Tower.

Art Deco

Just as Shanghai launched a city-wide building boom, Art Deco architecture exploded into the popular culture following the Exposition Internationale des Arts Décoratifs et Industriels Modernes in Paris in 1925. Shanghai's top architects embraced the new style, and designed thousands of examples. Soundly built of concrete and steel, the buildings were useful as well as elegant, and they served as workhorses for the city's rapidly expanding population. Many of the city's Art Deco classics have fallen to the wrecking ball, but many still remain, and today, Shanghai is one of the world's top showcases of this beloved style.

Art Deco

Classic Art Deco buildings are typified by simple vertical lines, linear elements, stepped forms and a lack of columns, which became obsolete with the invention of reinforced concrete. Other new materials like chrome, aluminium and stainless steel were also widely used in Art Deco, especially in decorative elements that often included chevrons and sunbursts. While some of Shanghai's Art Deco buildings have sweeping horizontal curves, most are vertical in form, with a pronounced central symmetry that climaxes in a dramatic peak at the apex of the building.

Fairmont Peace Hotel

20 Nanjing Road East, corner Nanjing Road and the Bund; tel: 10 800 714 1088; www.fairmont.com; Metro: Line 2, Nanjing East; Bus: 55, 910; map p.140 B3

The Peace Hotel, a green-crested landmark that sits on Shanghai's top piece of property – at the foot of Nanjing Road, on the Bund – is the best-known Art Deco building in Shanghai. Its opening

in 1929 came just after the discovery of King Tut's tomb in 1922, and the Peace has subtle Egyptian motifs, including a pair of sinuous cats near the apex. After spending years as a run-down hotel, the huge building was renovated in 2009, and reopened as the Fairmont Peace Hotel in early 2010.
SEE ALSO HOTELS, P.68

Grand Cinema

216 Nanjing Road West by Huanghe Road; tel: 6327-4260; 9am–11pm; Metro: line 1,2, 8, People's Square Station; map p.133 E3

The Grand Cinema, a László Hudec design that opened in the early 1930s, emerged in 2009 still sparkling from a faithful renovation that sought to restore or recreate many of its original Art Deco features. Its fine lobby, with its chrome and stainless-steel fittings, lotus-shaped decorations and sweeping curves of polished marble, does much to revive visions

Left: Fairmont Peace Hotel.

Architects from around the world flocked to Shanghai during its pre-war building boom, but two names tower above all others: the Hungarian genius László Hudec, and the British firm Palmer and Turner. More than 20 Hudec-designed buildings still stand in Shanghai, including two Art Deco masterpieces: the Park Hotel and the Grand Cinema. The prolific Palmer and Turner designed Customs House and the Hongkong and Shanghai Bank Building, the two grandest classical buildings on the Bund, and they also contributed many notable Art Deco classics, including the Fairmont Peace Hotel, the Metropole Hotel, Hamilton House, Broadway Mansions and the Old Bank of China Building.

of its illustrious past. Look closely at some of the details, and you can see the architect's distinctive logo.

Park Hotel

170 Nanjing Road West; tel: 6327 5225; www.parkhotel.com.cn; Metro: Lines 1, 2, People's Square; map p.134 A3

This stately structure opened with a bang in 1934, when it was the tallest building in Asia and hosted the most lavish parties in the hemisphere. The Art Deco lobby has long since disappeared, and the building badly needs cleaning, but its striking glazed-brick exterior is intact, and so are the simple straight lines of its signature Art Deco style, featuring four narrow strips that rise to the roof, buttressing the tower and highlighting its graceful vertical design. SEE ALSO HOTELS, P.70

Other Examples

Once you learn to recognise the style, Art Deco buildings will begin to pop up every-

where in Shanghai. Some are dramatic, like the two buildings that dominate the intersection of Jiangxi and Fuzhou roads: the **Metropole (or Xincheng) Hotel** and **Hamilton House**. Other impressive Art Deco exteriors include **Broadway Mansions Hotel**, the **Hengshan Picardie Hotel** and the **Grosvenor House Jinjiang Hotel**. Other structures are more subtle, like the breathtaking

Gascogne Apartments, at 1202 Huaihai Road Central With its subtle vertical symmetry, sweeping curves and simple decorative features, the Gascogne is the epitome of the Art Deco style. SEE ALSO HOTELS, P.71, 74, 75

Left: Park Hotel.
Right: Cathay Cinema.

Bars and Cafés

Bar and café culture is deeply ingrained in Shanghai, and drinking cocktails and beer, sunning on balconies, sipping tea and coffee, eating cakes and crème brûlées, and relaxing and socialising in intimate venues, are key elements of daily life. The narrow lanes, towering skyscrapers, Chinese teahouses and century-old villas of Shanghai provide a wealth of locations, and the options include coffee shops with freshly baked pastries, pubs with hand-crafted beers, dessert cafés with chocolate creations that are beyond rich, and many more. With so many tempting treats, the only real difficulty lies in making a choice.

The Bund

Glamour Bar
6/F, 20 Guangdong Road; tel: 6350 9988; www.m-the glamourbar.com; daily 5pm–late; Bus: 135, 145, 311; map p.140 B23
More than any other bar in Shanghai, the Glamour Bar evokes the atmosphere of the 1930s, although with modern peach-and-pink spotlighting and updated fancy drinks. Its old-school views of the Huangpu River, its plush and padded indolence and its fine service make this one of the city's best.

New Heights
3 Zhongshan Road East No.1, Three on the Bund Building; tel: 6321 0909; daily 11.30am–1am; Metro: Line 2, Nanjing East; map p.140 B1
No bar in Shanghai serves a fatter, juicier Martini than New Heights, on the top floor of Three on the Bund. The Bund has trendier watering holes, and cheaper ones, but New Heights has the ultimate trump card: an unbeatable view from its spacious, wraparound bal-

cony. What a sight – and what a Martini.
SEE ALSO RESTAURANTS, P.101

Old Town

Mid-Lake Teahouse (Huxinting Chashe)
257 Yuyuan Road; tel: 6373 6950; daily 5.30am–10pm; Bus: 932, 736; map p.135 C2
This famous 230-year-old teahouse, with its cheerful peaked roofs and cherry-red exteriors, perched on stilts above the bottle-green water of Yuyuan Lake, is a perfect place for a hot pot of pu'er or oolong tea. Choose your tea downstairs, then

head upstairs for the restful views of the willows and rooftops of nearby Yuyuan Garden.
SEE ALSO PARKS AND GARDENS, P.99

People's Park Area

Barbarossa Lounge
231 Nanjing Road West, inside Gate 7, People's Park; tel: 6318 0220; www.barbarossa.com.cn; daily 11am–late; Bus: 24, 738; map p.134 A2
The swish curtains, padded lounge chairs and Middle Eastern music and decor inspire visions of the *Arabian Nights* in this beautifully designed lounge bar. Its broad outdoor balcony overlooks the lotus ponds of People's Park, and offers views of the classic clock tower of the nearby Shanghai Art Museum, and the rocket-like spire of Tomorrow Square tower.

Xintiandi Area

Enoteca
58 Taicang Lu; tel: 5306 3400; www.enoteca.com.cn; daily 10am–1am; Metro: Line 1, Huangpi; map p.134 A1

Left and below left:
Glamour Bar.

Road; tel: 6393 1234 ext 6348;
Sun–Thur 6pm–1am, Fri–Sat
6pm–2am; Metro: Line 2, Nanjing East, then taxi; Bus: 33, 37;
map p.135 C4

Once – just once – it would
be fun to see somebody
jump into the circular outdoor hot tub that sits in the
middle of Vue Bar, a
vineyard-themed, two-
storey bar on the 33rd floor
of Hyatt on the Bund. Perhaps the patrons are too
distracted by the views of
Pudong and the Bund,
which are truly magnificent.
SEE ALSO WALKS AND VIEWS, P.127

Drinks are expensive in Shanghai bars, although bottled beer
in Chinese restaurants is cheap.
In a bar, expect to pay around
Rmb30 (US$4.50) for a stubby
bottle of Tsing Tao, about
Rmb40 for a bottle of imported
beer or a pint of draught lager,
and about Rmb65 for a pint of
Guinness. Mixed drinks start at
about Rmb40, and can escalate
rapidly from there.

Enoteca is a relaxed, non-
threatening wine bar that is
friendly and comfortable for
novices and experts alike. It
has a reasonable variety of
vintages, plus a good cheese-
board and a carefully crafted
menu of complementary
foods, presented in a refined
atmosphere of soft lighting
and postmodern decor.

Paulaner Brauhaus
House 19–20, North Block Xintiandi, Lane 181 Taicang Lu; tel:
6320 3935; www.bln.com.cn;
daily 11am–2pm, 5pm–late;
Metro: Line 1, Huangpi; map
p.134 A1

Home-brewed beer, pretzels
and sausages and other German comfort food, alfresco
tables that offer the best
people-watching in Xintiandi,
live music, a rollicking atmosphere and a non-stop parade
of German-themed parties
make this the most popular
bar in Xintiandi. (Also at 150
Fen Yang Road; tel: 6474 5700;
daily 11am–late; Metro: Line 1,
Changshu; Bus: 49, 96)

Hongkou and Suzhou Creek

Vue Bar
Hyatt on the Bund, 199
Huangpu Road by Wuchang

Nanjing Road West Area

Long Bar
2/F, Shanghai Centre, 1376 Nan-
jing Xi Lu, at the Portman Ritz-
Carlton; tel: 6279 8268; www.
ritzcarlton.com/en/Properties/
Shanghai; daily 11am–3am;
Metro: Line 2, Nanjing Road
West; map p.133 C2

A trip up the escalator into the
Long Bar, which hovers above
the open interiors of the
Shanghai Centre, is like
ascending into a space pod.
The bar itself is a long and
narrow space, always busy
and always cheerful, especially during one of its frequent
drinks or wine promotions.

Right: Barbarossa Lounge.

Left from top: the unparalleled skyline from Vue Bar *(see p.37)*; traditional teas and decadent coffees. **Right:** a fortune teller provides entertainment for customers.

Malone's American Cafe
255 Tongren Road; tel: 6247 2400; www.malones.com.cn; daily 11am–3am; Metro: Line 2, Nanjing Road West; Bus: 939; map p.132 C2

A broad and spacious two-storey eatery and bar, specialising in American pub grub and yankee sports – baseball, American football, basketball – is another long-running local institution. Book an outdoor table during good weather.

Woodstock
72 Tongren Lu, near Nanjing Xi Lu; tel: 3222 0031; daily 6pm–4am; Metro: Line 2, Nanjing Road West; Bus: 49, 57; map p.133 C1

A dark and cavernous space crawling with female patrons and abounding in lively conversation, Woodstock packs in the crowds with a can't-miss formula of '60s and '70s rock and roll, lively pool and foosball tables, and a perfect location smack in the middle of the Tong Ren Road nightlife strip.

While streetside tea cafés are still popular – they can be seen throughout the old concession streets, often with tables and teapots on the sidewalks – the latest phenomenon in Shanghai is **Taiwanese pearl milk tea**, or *zhen zhu nai cha*. This rich, sweet creation contains iced tea, milk, sugar and the tapioca 'pearls' themselves, which are sucked up through an extra-wide straw. It is normally served 'to go', although sit-down shops do exist.

Former French Concession North

Boxing Cat Brewery
82 Fuxing Road West, by Yongfu Road; tel: 6431 2091; www.boxingcatbrewery.com; Mon–Fri 5pm–2am, Sat–Sun 10am–2pm; Metro: Line 1, Changshu; Bus: 96, 113; map p.136 B3
The Boxing Cat brews American-style craft beers, with intense flavours of malt and hops, and serves them in a renovated villa on a quiet, tree-lined street. It has a good snack menu too, with nibbles, fries and various breads and dips to accompany its fine home brew.

Café Montmartre
66 Ulumuqi Road Central, corner of Chang Le: tel: 5158 9377; www.cafe-montmartre.com; daily 11am–midnight; Metro: Line 1, Changshu, then taxi; map p.136 B3
A French-style bakery and coffee shop that turns out excellent pastries and cakes, and good coffee too, in a big but thoughtful venue that pro-

vides intimacy, good views and a handful of outdoor tables. The staff are cheerful and efficient, and the French managers are ultra-helpful.

Citizen Café & Bar
222 Jinxian Road, near Shaanxi Road; tel: 6258 1620; www.citizenshanghai.com; 11am–12.30am; Metro: Line 1, Shaanxi; map p.133 D1
An intimate space with a bistro vibe, Citizen offers free wi-fi, which accounts for the lap-

tops perched on the tiny tables on the first floor. Though it gets noisy, particularly during after-work drinking hours, the café upstairs offers a retreat, along with a patio in warm weather, and a full range of menu items including soups and salads, sandwiches, hamburgers and pastas.

Manifesto
748 Julu Road, near Fumin Road; tel: 6289 9108; www.mesa-manifesto.com;

daily 10am–late; Bus: 49, 57; map p.137 C4

Manifesto is the perfect lounge bar: comfortable but not pretentious, busy but not packed, and stylish but not effete. It is a small but high-ceilinged space, with floor-to-ceiling windows and a standard bar in the middle, tables on one side, and Roman emperor-style lounge booths on the other.

Whisk Café

1250 Huaihai West Road, near Huating Road; tel: 5404 7770;

Left: classy drinks are everywhere in Shanghai, but pubs such as O'Malley's **(below)** provide a taste of home.

Tue–Sun 10.30am–11.30pm; Metro: Line 1, Changshu

The decadent chocolate desserts and hot cocoa with homemade marshmallows are the main draws here, but the quality soups, salads and pastas have also earned Whisk a strong following. Comfy booths near the front are prime seats, but they fill up quickly.

Former French Concession South

Abbey Road

45 Yueyang Lu, near Dongping Lu; tel: 6431 6787; www.abbey road-shanghai.com; Mon–Fri 4pm–2am, Sat–Sun 8.30am–2am; Metro: Line 1, Changshu; Bus 49, 96; map p.137 2C

It is hard to imagine a more relaxed and friendly bar and café than Abbey Road, and yes, it is named after the Beatles album. The bar lies in a convivial open room, while iron doors open onto a

bamboo-lined garden shaded by a towering green canopy of tree branches. Reasonably priced drinks, a Western menu cooked by a Swiss chef, and occasional live music add to the appeal.

The Beaver

28 Yueyang Road, near Dongping Road; tel: 6474 3216; daily 6pm–2am; Metro: Line 1, Changshu; Bus 49, 96; map p.137 2C

In a city full of ultra-fancy bars, the Beaver is a welcome antidote: small, cheerful and unadorned, this is a genuine neighbourhood local, with a dark, intimate vibe and a refrigerator filled with the best canned and bottled beers that Belgium, Britain, Germany and the US can brew.

Bulldog Shanghai

1 Wulumuqi South Road, near Dongping Road; tel: 6466 7878; www.bulldog-shanghai.com; Mon–Fri 5pm–2am, Sat–Sun 11am–2am; Metro: Line 1, Changshu; Bus: 1, 830; map p.136 C3

After struggling for a couple of years after its 2006 open-

ing, the Bulldog has found its niche: two-for-one drinks and attractive specials on beer and food every night of the week. It is a budget bar, although one with upscale interiors and a classy English pub ambience.

Cotton's

132 Anting Road, corner of Jianguo Road West; tel: 6433 7995; www.cottons-shanghai.com; Mon–Fri 11am–2am, Sat–Sun 11am–4am; Bus: 42, 236; map p.136 C2

Set in a beautiful old concession-era mansion with a broad, friendly patio and embraced by the protective boughs of the ever-present plane trees, this expat favourite is a real charmer. The cheerful presence of Cotton herself adds to the appeal, and so do the Chairman Mao cocktails and other unique spirited concoctions.

Kommune

Bldg 7, Lane 210 Taikang Road; tel: 6445 2416; Metro: Line 1, Shaanxi, then taxi; map p.137 E2

Shanghai is rich in **tea culture**, and its teahouses serve some of the finest teas in the world. Two of the most popular teas are partly fermented longjing oolong from the hills of nearby Hangzhou, and rich black pu'er tea from Yunnan province. The longjing oolong is mild, sweet and refreshing, with just a hint of caffeine, while the pu'er is rich, black and fully fermented, with an intense smoky taste and a pronounced caffeine kick.

Long before Taikang Road became the beehive of activity that it is today, Kommune was serving up coffee and sandwiches to the semi-bohemian art scene. Today, it boasts the liveliest patio seating in the neighbourhood and has added a brunch menu on Sundays. Here's an inside tip: check out the back door for additional seating.

La Creperie

1 Taojiang Road, near Fenyang Road; tel: 5465 9055; http://lacreperieshanghai.

spaces.live.com; 10.30am–late; Metro: Line 1, Changshu; Bus: 49, 96; map p.136 C2

The Brittany-born owner lends an air of authenticity to this fine café that specialises in sweet and savory crêpes. Try a buckwheat crêpe with camembert cheese and smoked ham, or a regular crêpe with stewed apple with butter and caramel, along with a Brittany hard cider – sweet or dry, the choice is yours – as an aperitif. In season, La Creperie offers specials on oysters and mussels flown in from France.

O'Malley's Irish Pub

42 Taojiang Road; tel: 6474 4533; www.omalleys-shanghai.com; daily 11am–2am; Metro: Line 1, Changshu; Bus 49, 96; map p.136 C2

The astroturf in the courtyard is tacky, and so is the new extension filled with picnic tables, but nothing can dent the popularity of O'Malley's. It is perpetually packed on weekend afternoons, and with its barbecue buffet, pints of Guinness, occasional live

music, rugby and cricket and other Commonwealth sports on TV, and central location, it simply shines brighter than any other pub in the neighbourhood.

Oscar's Pub

1377 Fuxing Road Central, corner of Bao Qing Road; tel: 6431 6528/6433 6806; daily 11am–1am; Metro: Line 1, Changshu; Bus: 1, 830; map p.137 C3

A bright and lively British-style pub, set in a two-storey villa with plenty of room for darts, live music, bar conversation and games of pool, along with a quieter patio for more intimate-minded patrons. Many people come here to unwind after work, and then settle in, eat and stay until midnight.

Park Tavern

840 Hengshan Lu, near Tianping Road; tel: 5465 9312; Mon–Thur 11am–2.30pm, Fri–Sun 11am–late; Metro: Line 1, Hengshan; Bus: 93; map p.136 B1

Housed in a renovated historic villa, and just across from Xujiahui Park, this English-style pub has four

levels, a spacious patio, and indoor and outdoor screens for international football, rugby and cricket matches.

Windows Scoreboard

3/F, 681 Huaihai Road Central; tel: 5382 7757; daily 5pm–late; Metro: Line 1, Huangpi; Bus: 1, 911; map p.137 D3

Windows has carved out a successful niche for itself: cheap beer and drinks, and plenty of them. Much loved by English teachers and Chinese students, Windows is the most Rmb-friendly pub in the city, and has a superior Huaihai Road location as well, along with abundant seating, pool and foosball and darts, and big screens perpetually filled with sports.

Zapata's

5 Hengshan Road; tel: 6474 6166/6433 4107; www.zapatas-shanghai.com; daily 5pm–2am, 4am on Wed, Fri and Sat; Metro: Line 1, Changshu; Bus: 1, 830; map p.136 C3

If you wish to see a ritual that rivals anything found in nature, head to Zapata's on a Wednesday night. That

Right: Chinese touches provide atmosphere at some bars, but Cloud Nine and Snow Bar **(below)** exemplify Shanghai's cutting-edge style.

would be ladies' night, when the place heaves and throbs with hundreds of patrons while the frantic staff pump out the beer and mixed drinks like there is no tomorrow. At other times Zapata's, a spacious bar with a barn-like main building and a roomy patio, is much more peaceful.

Pudong

Binjiang One Snow Bar
Youlong Garden, Shibu Jie, Fucheng Lu, Pudong, on the riverfront; tel: 5877 7500; www.bln.com.cn; daily 5pm–1am; Bus: 81, 86; map p.135 D3

Don your jacket – or they'll give you one at the door – and head into the sub-zero chill of this frozen cave, where frosty bottles of vodka and blue neon lights add to the icy ambience. The vodka is always ice-cold, and most of the

patrons are too, making this a perfect retreat on a hot summer day.

Cloud Nine
87/F, Jinmao Tower, in Grand Hyatt Hotel; tel: 5049 1234, ext 8778; http://shanghai.grand.hyatt.com; Mon–Thur 5pm–1am, Fri 5pm–2am, Sat–Sun 11am–2am; Metro: Line 2, Dongchang; map p.135 E3
Once the highest bar in the world, it is no longer; the new highest bar is the Living

Room bar at the Park Hyatt *(see below)*, just a few metres away through the moist Shanghai air. But Cloud Nine is still plenty high, with towering views of the Bund and Puxi, and its two levels of seating guarantee good sightlines from every table.

Living Room at Park Hyatt
87/F, 100 Century Avenue; tel: 6888 1234; Metro: Line 2, Dongchang; map p.135 E3

It is a bargain, if you think about it: a trip to the top of the Shanghai World Financial Centre Tower costs Rmb100 to Rmb 150, but here, just a few floors below, a cocktail is Rmb80, and the views are absolutely free. The sparkling tip of the Jinmao Tower is so close you could almost touch it, and beyond that lies the vast and throbbing city of Shanghai, in all its glory.

Children

Children serve as a cross-cultural ice-breaker in China. You will often hear smaller children referred to as *xiao bao bei* – or precious little treasures. Despite this adoration of children, Shanghai is not well geared for child-friendly or family activities, although this is changing as the population grows more prosperous. For example, hotel restaurants now have play areas for children that are staffed with caretakers so parents can enjoy their meal and after 20 years of negotiation, Disney has at last been given permission to build a Magic Kingdom-style theme park in Pudong. It is expected to open in 2015.

Amusement Parks

Dino Beach
78 Xinzhen Road, Minhang; tel: 6478 3333; www.dinobeach. com.cn; June–Sept Mon 2–10pm, Wed and Sun 10am–10pm, Tue, Thur and Fri 10am–midnight; admission; Metro: Line 1, Xinzhuang; Bus: 763, 173 to park entrance
This vast, kid-friendly water park features a wave pool, artificial beach, water slides, tube rides and three kiddie pools.

Jinjiang Amusement Park
201 Hongmei Road; tel: 5420 0844; www.jjlysh.com; 8.45am–5pm; admission; Metro: Line 1, Jinjiang Park; Bus: 50, 131, 704
Opened in 1986 by the Jinjiang Group, this amusement park is a bit dated but has lately been sprucing itself up. Its signature ride is a giant

ferris wheel that offers eye-watering views of southern Shanghai.

Animal Attractions

Changfeng Ocean World
Gate 4, 21 Changfeng Park, 451 Daduhe Road; tel: 5281 8888/ 6286 6399; admission; www.oceanworld.com.cn (Chinese only); 8.30am–5pm summer, 9am–5pm winter;

admission; Bus: 44
Located in northern Shanghai within one of the city's oldest parks, Ocean World features regular aquatic shows including belugas and sea lions, as well as a penguin colony and a shark tank.

Shanghai Aquarium
158 Yincheng North Road; tel: 5877 9988; www.aquarium.

> Unless otherwise specified, children under 1.2m (3ft 11ins) enjoy free admission. This includes buses, the Metro and park entry fees.

Left: kids will also love the Shanghai Science and Technology Museum (see p.85).

has also gained a following among the picnic set, who enjoy the grounds in the spring and autumn.

Arts and Crafts

Creative Workshop
3/F, 388 Grand Gateway, 1 Hongqiao Road; tel: 6447 9273; daily noon–8pm; admission; Metro: Line 1, Xujiahui; map p.137 E4

This cosy workshop has a fun variety of arts and crafts for children, as well as traditional Chinese pastimes such as paper cutting and black ink watercolour painting.

House of Barbie
550 Huaihai Central Road; tel: 6171 6036; www.barbie shanghai.com

Yes, Barbie turned 50 in 2009, and that same year the plastic princess opened her first Barbie flagship store. This frilly pink palace has a spiral stairwell that displays 800 Barbies in hot pink outfits, and a design centre where kids can design their own Barbies, and a fashion runway where they can have their photos taken dressed in a favourite Barbie outfit.

Although disposable nappies are becoming more popular, many Chinese dress their babies in split pants, which allows them to relieve themselves at will, in public, without soiling their clothes.

---

sh.cn; Metro: Line 2, Lujiazui; map p.135 D4

This new, Singapore-designed extravaganza at the base of the Pearl Oriental Tower is a first-rate entertainment filled with fine displays and plentiful signs in several languages. The signature exhibit is a 155m (500ft) long underwater observation tunnel, where sharks pass overhead displaying fearsome saw-toothed smiles.

Shanghai Wild Animal Park
178 Liukou Road, Sanzao Town, Nanhui District; tel: 5803 7621; daily 8am–5pm; admission; Bus: 2, from the Shanghai Municipal Stadium

This spacious reserve has a Jurassic Park setup where guests board buses and ride through animal compounds. Keep the windows closed, as the lions, attracted by dangling food, leap close to the windows. Other enclosures feature leopards, tigers and bears.

Shanghai Zoo
2381 Hongqiao Road; tel: 6268 7775; daily 7am–6pm; admission; Bus: 505, 831, 911

This zoo's giant panda and monkey exhibits really attract the crowds, as does the new crocodile house. It

Left: Jinjiang Amusement Park. **Right:** under water at Shanghai Aquarium.

Churches and Temples

Shanghai's temples are not as colourful or vibrant as those in Taiwan, Singapore, Hong Kong, and elsewhere in the Chinese diaspora. But the old religions are beginning to return, and the traditions associated with Taoism, Confucianism and Buddhism are slowly becoming more common. Western churches have undergone a similar progression, and while most are generally quite empty, they do fill up with worshippers on Sundays, and are overflowing on holidays like Easter and Christmas Eve.

Old Town

City God Temple (Cheng Huang Miao)

249 Fang Bang Road Central; tel: 6386 5700; daily 8.30am–4.30pm; admission; Metro: Line 8, Laoximen, then taxi; map p.135 C2

City God temples, normally featuring fierce gods who protect the city from evil, are generally among the busiest Taoist temples in a given town, and Shanghai's version is no exception. Its main deity is Huo Guang, a local military hero, but there are many lesser gods, and worshippers burn incense, light candles and make offerings, as they ask them for favours.

St Francis Xavier Church (Dong Jia Du Lu Catholic Church)

Most of the Chinese temples in Shanghai charge admission, but the ticket prices are quite modest, usually Rmb5 to Rmb10. Most are also surrounded with stands selling souvenirs, along with offerings for the gods, such as incense and candles.

185 Dong Jia Du Road, near Wanyu Road; tel: 6378 7214; Services: Mon–Sat 7am, Sun Mass (English) 12.30, 4.30pm; Metro: Line 4, Nanpu Bridge, then taxi; map p.139 E3

Designed and built by Spanish Jesuits in 1853, this old structure is a fine example of Spanish colonial architecture, with graceful arched rooms, sturdy pillars, and bas-reliefs inside that display some East–West religious fusion, such as Chinese couplets and lotus flowers.

People's Park Area

Moore Memorial Church (Mu'en Tang)

316 Xizang Road Central; tel:

6322 5069; Services (Chinese only): 7, 9.30am, 2, 7pm; Metro: Line 1, 2, People's Square; map p.134 B1

The splendid facade of this Gothic red-brick church, built in 1997, expanded in the 1930s, and underwent a year-long renovation in 2009. It is a People's Park landmark.

Hongkou and Suzhou Creek

Ohel Moshe Synagogue (Moxi Hui Tang)

62 Changyang Road, near Zhoushan Road; tel: 6512 6669; daily 9am–4.30pm; admission; Metro: Line 4, Dalian

In the 1930s, Shanghai was a haven for Jews fleeing Europe, and the remarkable history of that migration is on display here through a series of photographs and descriptions. It is not longer a functioning synagogue, but is fascinating nonetheless.

Nanjing Road West Area

Jade Buddha Temple (Yu Fo Si)

170 An Yuan Road, near Jiangning Road; tel: 6266 3668; daily 8am–4.30am; admission; Metro:

Left: wish tree at Long Hua Temple.

Western Shanghai

Long Hua Si

2853 Long Hua Road; tel: 6456 6085; daily 7am–4.30pm; admission; Metro: Line 3, Longcao

If you visit just one temple in Shanghai, make it Long Hua. It is famous for its octagonal, seven-storey wood-and-brick pagoda, which dates from the Southern Song Dynasty (AD 960–1279), although the extensive grounds and Buddhist deities are also eminently worthwhile.

Xujiahui Catholic Church, formerly St Ignatius Cathedral

158 Pu Xi Road, near Caoxi North Road; tel: 6438 0930; daily Mass 6, 7am, Sun Mass 6, 7, 10am, 6pm

The twin spires of this redbrick cathedral are prominent landmarks of Shanghai's most famous Western church. The revamped interiors feature new stained-glass windows.

Line 4, Zhenping, then taxi; map p.132 B4

Busloads of tourists routinely visit this site in northern Shanghai, primarily to admire the two truly beautiful white Buddhas, one seated and one reclining, that are each carved from a single piece of super-lustrous Burmese jade.

Jing'an Temple

1686 Nanjing Road West; tel: 6256 6366; daily 7.30am–5pm; admission; Metro: Line 2, Jinan Temple; map p.132 B1

This cherry-red temple sits on a very visible site that is more than 1,000 years old. The chief attraction is a 3.5 tonne Ming Dynasty bell, though the smaller stone Buddhas from Chinese antiquity are equally interesting.

Former French Concession South

International Church (Guo Ji Li Bai Tang)

53 Hengshan Road, near Wulumuqi Road; tel: 6437 6576;

Services: Wed (Chinese) 7.30am and 7pm, Sun (Chinese) 7.30am, (Chinese with English translator) 10am, (English) 2 and 4pm; Metro: Line 1, Hengshan; map p.136 C2

This pretty 1920s-era ivy-covered brick building is the most used Protestant church in Shanghai, especially during the 4pm Sunday services for foreign passport-holders.

Above left: a statue of Confucius. **Right:** Jade Buddha Temple.

Custom-Made in Shanghai

O ne of the real delights for any shopper in Shanghai is the range of custom-made items that can be bought for a fraction of the prices charged elsewhere. Anything from hardwood furniture to jewellery can be made to specifications. Labour is inexpensive, so you can invest more in quality material. Make it clear from the beginning that workmanship is of the greatest importance. Other tips include bringing a photo of a desired piece, being specific about details, and allowing time for adjustments if the result is below par.

Cashmere

There are a number of small shops around the French Concession that will machine-knit-to-order cashmere sweaters. Many feature the English word 'cashmere' on the front window, and will have a number of sweaters and scarves on display to serve as samples for custom-made items or for purchase.

Bennie's Cashmere House

105 Wukang Road, near Fuxing West Road, tel: 5465 1193; daily 10am–7pm; map p.136 B3
The wool from this store is sourced in China, then exported to Italy where it is dyed and spun, and the result is a beautifully soft cashmere yarn. The knitting takes place in a factory off site, and may take up to three weeks to a month, depending on the complexity of the desired design and availability of the yarn colours. A thin, long-sleeved V-neck sweater with no ribbing goes for about Rmb800.

Cashmere House

147 Fuxing West Road; tel: 6431 5177; daily 10am–6pm; map p.136 B3
Also 140 Nanchang Road, near Sinan Road; tel: 6384 9582; 11am–6.30pm; map p.137 E4
This outlet has two locations in the French Concession, with the one on Nanchang Road somewhat larger, so it tends to have more items on display. Discounted sales take place in the summer, when demand is low. Men's, women's and children's sweaters as well as scarves and socks can be made to measure.

Furniture

Elm Workshop

1501 Jinsui Road, off Jinhai Road, Pudong; tel: 1368 1642 555/1368 1684 222; www.elm

Above: Elm Workshop.
Right: Hu & Hu Sofa.

Most establishments will require a deposit. The amount is usually a fraction of the total negotiated price (Rmn100 for an Rmb500 piece, for example). Be sure to check for flaws and fit when picking up the goods before paying the final balance.

Left: Illudeco lighting shop *(see p.50).*

daily 10am–7pm; www.hu-hu-sofa.com; map p.136 B3
Launched by two sisters-in-law, the original Hu & Hu continues to sell refurbished Chinese wooden furniture in the western part of the city (No. 8, Lane 1885, Caobao Road; tel: 3431 1212), but this location in the French Concession specialises in upholstered sofas and chairs, ranging from fine fabrics to leather.

Jewellery

Angel
288 Fuyou Road, First Asia 3/F, stall No. 3005; tel: 6311 0230; map p.135 C2
Take the escalator past the gold jewellery on the first floor and the sleeping staff and jade carvings on the second floor, and arrive amid dozens of stalls selling strings of pearls and other semi-precious stones and beads. Although any number of these stalls will string up necklaces and bracelets while you wait or sell the samples on display, Angel is recommended for her straightforward negotiating tactics.

workshop.com
A favourite among expats living in Shanghai for its service and English-speaking skills, this workshop run by an American and his Taiwanese wife can replicate a favourite antique or create a new piece from your imagination or from a catalogue, using a variety of wood ranging from ash and elm to exotic, plantation-grown imports such as teak. Catalogues and samples in the showroom offer plenty of options, and they've recently

Keep price negotiations friendly. Unlike vendors of fake watches, these businesses offer unique products and have a standard rate. Ask for their best price, but don't expect them to knock the asking price in half. Instead, they might round off a few yuan to an even number.

launched a new line of children's furniture.

Hu & Hu Sofa
201 Anfu Road; tel: 5403 9867;

'**Painter's Street**' on 212 Wending Road near Nandan Road has about 30 studios that will reproduce oil paintings. Have your portrait done or bring in a photo of a favourite piece – or a photo of yourself – to have painted.

Passion Bijoux

2/F, Shanghai Hongqiao International Pearl City, 3721 Hongmei Road; tel: 138 1632 4086

Although called Pearl City, this complex offers much more, including turquoise, amethyst, garnet and tiger-eye among others. Most vendors on the second floor feature both finished products and beads sold by the string. Passion Bijoux caters to a foreign crowd, which may account for slightly higher prices.

Lamps

Illudeco

450 Xiangyang South Road; tel: 6471 8137; www.illudeco. com; Mon–Sat 9am–6pm; map p.137 D2

This small studio, located in the French Concession, brings together the works of a number of locally based designers from overseas. It features a wide range of custom-made lamps and lampshades, and simple styles can be completed in seven days.

Light Scene

162 Yinzhu Road, near Hongbaoshi Road; tel: 6295 7000; daily 9.30am–6pm

Specialising in customised wrought-iron lamps, often covered with rice paper or silk, this store features scores of options for those looking for a unique lighting piece. The showroom has a variety of kimono-shaped desk lamps, floor candleholders and other decorative wrought-iron pieces. English-speaking Lucia is most helpful.

Leather Shoes and Handbags

A number of small leather studios will measure your feet and then stitch handmade shoes to order. Depending on complexity of the design, completion usually takes about seven to 10

days. Some studios will also make handbags and belts to specifications.

Mr Billy's Hand Made Shoes

1238 Changle Road; tel: 6248 4881; www.billyshoes.com; map p.136 B3

Billy Wang has over 20 years of shoemaking experience, and is well known among Shanghai's expat residents. Prices range from Rmb900 to Rmb1,300 for men's shoes and Rmb650 to Rmb950 for women's shoes. Boots range from Rmb650 to Rmb1,300.

Will's Hand Made Shoes

141–1 Fuxing West Road; tel: 6433 6387; Mon–Sat 10am–7pm, Sun noon–7pm; map p.136 B3

Customers can choose from a range of leather from China, Spain and Italy from this workshop. Men's shoes range from Rmb960 for Chinese leather to Rmb1,360 for Italian leather. Women's shoes are between Rmb200 and Rmb700.

Yanye Hand Made Shoes

893 Huashan Road; tel: 131 6270 5506; daily noon–9pm

This establishment on the

Above and left: Light Scene boutique. **Above right:** Phonepha. **Right:** Will's Hand Made Shoes.

Good neighbourhoods for finding tailors include around five-star hotels and along Maoming Road between Nanchang and Changle. Many offer decent service, but insist on the finest quality of materials and examine their samples closely to check for quality of workmanship.

edge of the French Concession has a number of catalogues to give an idea of the different styles possible.

Men's and Women's Wear

Chen Xiong Zhi Yi

13 Dongping Road, near Hengshan Road, tel: 6472 2898; daily 10am–7pm; map p.136 C3
Three Shanghai-based tailors hand-make women's wool suits, dresses and skirts with fabric imported largely from Japan. Completion takes about 15 days, though rush jobs can take a week.

Dave's Tailor

No. 6, Lane 288, Wuyuan Road; tel: 5404 0001; www.tailordave. com; daily 10am–7pm; map p.136 B3
Highly recommended by residents of Shanghai, this Dave's Tailor is not to be confused with the Dave's Tailor in the Shanghai Centre. Dave's offers reliable high-end quality for made-to-measure men's suits and shirts.

Feel Shanghai

Room 110, No. 3, Lane 210, Taikang Road; tel: 5465 4519; daily 10am–8pm; map p.137 E2
Designer Lee Jialing specialises in hand-sewn traditional Chinese clothing for men and women. The store has a limited but high-quality selection of Chinese and Thai silks to choose from, ranging from traditional brocade to modern patterned fabrics. Photos are on hand to give an idea of the variety of styles available. Depending upon the complexity of design selected, items can be completed in a week to 10 days.

Phonepha

7–2 Dongping Road; tel: 5465 2468; www.thefrenchtailor.com; map p.136 C3
French-born Guillaume and his Vietnamese wife Phonepha have been importing top-of-the-line European textiles to China since 1997, specialising in men's suits and shirts. Their prices may be higher than others', but their attention to detail and superb workmanship – and the stratospheric thread counts – make Phonepha exceptional.

Essentials

For non-Chinese-speakers, Shanghai is quite easy to navigate. Chinese street signs include the romanisation or *pinyin* of the Chinese names as well as arrows pointing north, south, east and west. Tourist maps are easy to read and include major attractions, as well as romanised street names. English is not widely spoken outside five-star hotels and restaurants, but it is becoming more common. The Shanghainese have long been considered very open to outside influences and visitors, and they are generally unfazed by the presence of foreigners on their streets.

Embassies

Australia
22/F, Citic Square, 1168 Nanjing Road West; tel: 5292 5500; www.china.embassy.gov.au; Metro: Line 1, between Jinan Temple and Nanjing West; Bus: 41, 738; map p.133 D2

Canada
Suite 604, Shanghai Centre, 1376 Nanjing Road West; tel: 6279 8400; www.shanghai.gc.ca; Metro: Line 1, Jinan Temple; map p.133 C2

New Zealand
1605–1607A, 989 Changle Road; tel: 5407 5858; www.nzembassy.com; Metro: Line 1, Changshu; map p.136 B3

United Kingdom
Suite 301, Shanghai Centre, 1376 Nanjing Road West; tel: 3279 2000; www.ukinchina.fco.gov.uk; Metro: Line 2, Jinan Temple; map p.133 C2

United States
Main Consulate Building: 1469 Central Huaihai Road; tel: 6433 6880; American Citizen Services: 8/F, Westgate Mall, 1038 Nanjing West Road; tel: 3217 4650, after-hours emergencies only tel: 6433 3936; shanghai.usconsulate.gov; Metro: Line 2, between Jinan Temple and Nanjing West; map p.136 C3

Emergency Numbers
The police have a foreign translator on hand 24/7, so it is the best number to call in an emergency.
Ambulance: 120
Fire: 119
Police: 110

Gay and Lesbian
Acceptance of the gay and lesbian community in Shanghai has been tentative. Shanghai LGBT (shanghailgbt@yahoogroups.com) hosts events in a handful of the city's gay and lesbian bars.

Health
Healthcare in Shanghai is adequate, and some hospitals have priority care sections that have English-speaking personnel. Other hospitals only treat foreigners in emergencies. Visitors to Shanghai should have health insurance that covers repatriation expenses.

You should bring all required medications during your visit, whether over-the-counter or prescription. The Centre for Disease Control in the United States recommends the following vaccines for travellers to Shanghai: Hepatitis A and B, Japanese encephalitis (for those travelling to rural areas for four weeks or more) and rabies. For more information, check their website: www.cdc.gov.

Children's Medical Centre, Foreigners' Ward
19/F, 1678 Dongfang Road, near Pujiang Road, Pudong; tel: 5839 5238; Mon–Fri 8am–7.30pm, Sat–Sun 8am–4pm; Metro: Line 6, Shanghai Children's Medical Centre

Huashan Hospital
VIP Section, 19/F, 12 Wulumuqi Middle Road, near Huashan Road; tel: 6248 9999 ext 9998 or 5288 9998; www.huashan.org.cn; Mon–Fri 8.30am–5pm, emergency only Sat–Sun 8.30am–9.30pm; Bus: 148, 93

Left: recent recruits at the Police Training Centre.

Post and Telephones

Shanghai's main post office is located at 395 Suzhou North Road (tel: 6393 6666), and international mail counters are open from 7am–7pm. Every neighbourhood has at least one post office open generally from 8.30am–5.30pm.

The country code for China is 86 and city code for Shanghai is 21, or 021 when dialling from inside the country. Most mobile phone-users with roaming facility will be able to hook up with the GSM 900 network, with the exception of those from Japan. Public phones require a prepay card; calls are Rmb0.20 for three minutes.

Tipping

Locals do not tip, and service professionals outside five-star hotels don't expect tips.

Visa Information

Apply for visas in your home country prior to arriving in China. Hong Kong is also a convenient alternative. A single-entry, 30-day visa is usually provided for those with passports with a minimum of six months' validity. Those transiting through Shanghai can enter the city visa-free for 24 hours or 48 hours, but check with your embassy. Double-entry or multiple-entry visas are more expensive and more difficult to obtain.

The entire country operates on Beijing time, which is eight hours ahead of Greenwich Mean Time (GMT), and there is no daylight savings time. Having a single time zone in such a large country means that on the east coast, the sun rises very early.

Parkway Health – Shanghai Centre
Suite 203, West Retail Plaza, Shanghai Centre, 1376 Nanjing West Road; 24-hour hotline: 6445 5999; www.parkwayhealth.cn (five other locations listed online); Mon–Fri 9am–7pm, Sat–Sun 9am–5pm; Metro: Line 2, Jinan Temple; map p.133 C2

Information

Shanghai Tourist Hotline
Tel: 962 020; 24 hours
An excellent service that provides English-speaking assistance and information on all tourism-related topics.

Internet

Most business-class hotels have either in-room wi-fi or ports for high-speed Internet connections or at a business centre. Many cafés and small restaurants offer wi-fi for the cost of a coffee.

Media

Shanghai has two daily English-language newspapers. **The Shanghai Daily** (www.shanghaidaily.com) is published locally. **The China Daily** (www.chinadaily.com.cn) is the national newspaper published in Beijing. The English edition of the Chinese-language **People's Daily** is available online at english. peopledaily.com.cn. Foreign newspapers and magazines are available only at the city's four- and five-star hotels.

Free English-language publications that feature restaurant and entertainment listings are **City Weekend** (www.cityweekend.com.cn) and **That's Shanghai** (www.thats sh.com). They can be found at many bars and restaurants.

Money

Chinese currency is called the yuan (CNY) or renminbi (Rmb). One renminbi is colloquially called *kuai*, and is divided into 10 mao, or jiao, which is further divided into 10 fen.

Major currencies can be changed at hotels, but you must be a registered guest, or at Bank of China and ICBC, which requires a passport. Be sure to keep the foreign exchange receipt, which is required to change your remaining renminbi back to your home currency.

Expo 2010

The world's tallest, longest, fastest – Shanghai is no stranger to hyperbole. And on 1 May 2010, the city will host the grandest World Expo of all time, a six-month extravaganza that will feature more than 200 countries and attract 70 million visitors from China and around the world. The ambitious US$4 billion project is located on a huge, 5.28-sq-km (2-sq-mile) tract of land that covers 8.3km (5 miles) of prime Huangpu River waterfront. When it closes on 31 October 2010, Expo 2010 will have replaced docks and factories with offices, restaurants and retail.

Time in the Spotlight

Not all World Expos are equal. The last major exposition was held in 2005 in Aichi, Japan, and it ran for six months and attracted 22 million visitors. The three-month 'Water Expo' in Zaragoza, Spain, held in 2008, attracted 6 million spectators. But some World Expos are dramatic successes that become part of the cultural landscape.

These include the 1939 New York World's Fair, which introduced television to the world, and the equally famous 1889 Paris Expo, which showcased the brand-new Eiffel Tower. These famous fairs were landmark events that catapulted their host cities to further global fame.

Shanghai hopes to accomplish the same mission with Expo 2010, cementing its image as one of the world's top cities and displaying its virtues to the world.

Around the World

The city has spared no effort or expense in its effort to create one of the greatest World Expos of all time. It moved more than 10,000 families into newly built housing in Pudong, and relocated several hundred factories, including an enormous shipyard that employed 10,000 workers.

The effort appears to have worked: the amount of global interest in Expo 2010 is staggering, as more than 200 countries, many with the support of corporate sponsors, built pavilions. Most of the pavilions are designed to create a single, sharp image of a country. The **United Arab Emirates pavilion**, for example, is constructed of rose-coloured steel and shaped like a curving, crescent sand

Above: a bird's-eye view of the Expo site. **Right:** the Chinese pavilion at Expo 2010.

Tickets are available for single days and evening admissions, while group tickets, and three-day and seven-day passes, are also available. See the official site, http://en.expo2010.cn, for more information.

Left: Mascot for Expo 2010.

pavilion designed to look like a bird's nest, a tribute to Beijing's Olympic Stadium.

France, meanwhile, will unveil a 'floating pavilion' surrounded by water like a Monet painting; the **Canada pavilion** will feature Cirque du Soleil; and **Hong Kong** will pitch in with a modernistic metallic structure with transparent exteriors, and a replica of a wetland park on the inside. It will be near the landmark 'oriental crown' Chinese Pavilion, a magnificent replica of a traditional wooden structure, built on a grand scale.

With a few exceptions, including the Chinese Pavilion and the large, dome-shaped Performance Centre, all the pavilions will be removed at the end of the fair, to make way for more development. Some have been sold, and will be rebuilt in provincial capitals around China, while others, remarkable and expensive though they may be, are destined for the dustbin of architectural history.

> The 60m (200ft) tall **China Pavilion** towers high above all the other buildings at Expo 2010, and this is not by accident: all other countries have a height limit of just 20m (65ft).

dune. The **Danish pavilion** will import the Little Mermaid from Copenhagen and surround it with water from the seas of Denmark, while the Italian pavilion is inspired by a Chinese game of pick-up sticks, where 20 to 30 sticks are tossed on a table.

The list goes on: the **Australian pavilion** will look like Ayers Rock; the **Malaysian pavilion** will have the sharp, graceful peaks of a traditional Malaysian dwelling; **Thailand** will build a large-scale replica of a traditional Thai temple; while **Brazil** will present a

Fashion

Fashion in China has gone from Mao jackets to Prada dresses and Gucci bags almost overnight, and cutting-edge Shanghai is the country's fashion capital. It has been said the Shanghainese would rather look good than eat well, and market surveys rank Shanghai residents as the top consumers of clothing and beauty products in China. The fashion scene has so far been dominated by international brands, but increasingly, as young fashion mavens consider fashion as a form of self-expression rather than a mirror of magazine layouts, local designers have begun to make an impression on the streets of Shanghai.

Designers

Shanghai is beginning to take shape as a fashion centre, as its young designers go abroad for schooling, and the city attracts an increasing number of international designers.

Chloe Chen

2/F, 174 Xiangyang South Road; tel: 5465 7275; daily 10am–9pm; www.chloechen.com; Metro: Line 1, Shaanxi; Bus: 42, 45, 236; map p.137 D3

This Taiwanese designer began her career designing shoes that were made in Korea. She has continued to source from Korea and has since added casual-wear clothing to her stores, which also include hand-picked designer lines that are typified by a fun yet sophisticated flair.

Every year, the Shanghai government sponsors **Shanghai Fashion Week** in an attempt to shift the city's reputation from a manufacturing base to a hub of creativity and design prowess. It invites dozens of designers from both home and abroad to showcase their talent.

Feel Shanghai

Room 110, No. 3, Lane 210, Taikang Road; tel: 5465 4519/ 6466 8065; daily 10am–8pm; Metro: Line 1, Shaanxi, then taxi; Bus: 24, 236, 864; map p.137 E2

Designer Lee Jialing specialises in custom-made and off-the-rack traditional Chinese clothing for men and women. While the selection of fabrics available may not equal the quantity found at the fabric markets, the quality and range are well considered. Styles are traditional with an updated twist.

Han Feng Design

Jinjiang Hotel, 59 Maoming South Road, Grosvenor House, Suite 3EF; tel: 6472 7202; Mon–Fri 9.30am–6pm; Metro: Line 1, Shaanxi; Bus: 26, 146; map p.137 D3

This Nanjing native's interest in fashion began with a stint working at Bloomingdales in New York. She began designing scarves and accessories and has gone on to create elaborate evening gowns and whimsical artistic pieces. She has also created costumes for the Met's production of *Madame Butterfly* in New York.

Above: Feel Shanghai.
Right: Urban Tribe (see p.58).

Left: Chloe Chen boutique.

Jooi Design

Studio 201, 2/F, Lane 210, Taikang Road; tel: 6473 6193; daily 10am–6pm; Metro: Line 1, Shaanxi, then taxi; Bus: 24, 236, 864; map p.137 E2

Danish designer Trina Targett has established a name for herself in her adopted home with her leather and fine silk embroidered handbags and scarves. She has recently expanded her collection to include women's clothing and housewares.

Shiatzy Chen

9 on the Bund, 9 Zhongshan

Heyan'er

284 Anfu Road, next to Shanghai Dramatic Arts Centre; tel: 5404 8818; www.heyaner.com; daily 10am–10.30pm; Metro: Line 1, Changshu; Bus: 15, 93, 94; map p.136 B3

Natural fibres such as cotton, linen and silk are highlighted in this Beijing-born designer's work, which is strongly influenced by traditional Chinese silhouettes and motifs. Men's and women's casual wear as well as more elegant attire are available both off the rack and made to measure.

Innovative Design

Shanghai Mart, 2299 Yanan West Road; tel: 6236 6888; Metro: Line 2, Loushanguan, then taxi

Opened at the end of 2008, this boutique is located in a unique spot, a huge and cavernous trading centre. Operated by the Shanghai Mart, Innovative Design features the works of Shanghai's top names in fashion design, including Zhang Zhaoda and Wu Xuekai. Collections include an eclectic selection of pieces, from denim to evening gowns.

A subset of the Shanghai fashion scene is its dozens of lavish, high-profile **wedding stores**. Couples rent elaborately designed (and usually matching) formal wear, sometimes outfits from history, for about Rmb150 a day, have their hair and makeup professionally done, and pose for a series of photographs that are blown up and put on display at their wedding banquets, and then collected in an album. Tourists are welcome as well, and at the end of the process they will have a unique souvenir.

Twenty years ago, the only consumers of luxury brands in China were businessmen who bought expensive watches and pens to impress their clients. Today, that role has been taken over by career women. Although the market continues to be largely accessories (think handbags and shoes), luxury brands are investing heavily in China, banking on the rising tide of aspirational shoppers who grew up with knock-off bags and are now reaching for the real thing.

East Road; tel: 6321 9155; Unit D, 59 Maoming South Road, by Changle Road; tel: 5466 1266; Metro: Line 2, Nanjing East; Bus: 20; map p.140 B2

High-end Taiwan-born fashion designer Shiatzy Chen combines subtle Chinese design motifs with a Western sense of style. Items range from full-length evening gowns to crisp tailored shirts, and include a range of men's clothing as well as housewares.

Urban Tribe

133 Fuxing West Road; tel: 6433 5366; daily 10am–10pm; Bus: 96, 113, 548; map p.136 B3
This boutique is strongly influenced by the cultures of India, Burma and China's western provinces. Men's and women's fashions are typified by muted colours and flowing cotton and linen fabrics. Urban Tribe also fea-

tures simple and elegant jewellery featuring semi-precious stones and silver, as well as tea, stationery and black-and-white photos of the people of the Himalayas.

Younik

18 Bund, 18 Zhongshan East Road; tel: 6323 8688; daily 10am–10pm; Metro: Line 2, Nanjing East; map p.140 B3
Setting itself apart from the international big guns on the Bund like Ermenegildo Zegna, Cartier and Giorgio Armani, Younik features Shanghai designer wear. Highlights include pieces from Lu Kun, Jenny Ji and Zhang Da, whose O T-shirts look like oversized felt discs when laid flat and are loose-fitted garments when worn.

Browsing Neighbourhoods

Changle Road

Stores along Changle Road from Maoming Road eastwards are known for featuring budding Shanghai designer

For the most part, young Chinese women consider the *chipao*, the traditional Chinese dress, a relic of the past worn only by waitresses. But by putting a modern spin with unconventional fabrics or patterns, dressmakers are beginning to foster a new appreciation of the *chipao*.

close-up glimpse into the daily lives of the locals. Some interesting fashion destinations are **inSh** (200 Taikang Road; tel: 6466 5249), **NEST** (Studio 201, Lane 210, Taikang Road; tel: 6466 9524) and **La Vie** (No. 7, Lane 210, Taikang Road; tel: 6445 3585), which features fashions by promising designers **Jenny Ji** and **Helen Lee**.

SEE ALSO SHOPPING, P.117

Xinle Road

Tree-lined Xinle Road, from Changshu to Shaanxi roads, features dozens of small boutiques that make for an easy afternoon of browsing. Those with treasure-hunting skills may be rewarded with designer brand items (some may have their labels cut off, so know what you're looking for) at sharply discounted prices.

items. Stores that have developed a following among the local fashion crowd include **Estune** (139–19 Changle Road, near Ruijin Road; tel: 5306 9973), **Even Penniless** (139–3 Changle Road; tel: 5306 0466), **Wang Yiyang** and **Da Yuan Jing** (149–21 Changle Road; tel: 6385 1471), which means big round mirror.

Maoming Road

This street used to be lined with scores of *chipao* tailors, and while the number has dwindled in recent years, there are still a few around from Huaihai Road to Fuxing Road. One such establishment is **Jin Zhi Yu Ye** (72 Maoming Road), which is known for its quality.

Shaanxi Road

Shoe-o-holics will enjoy browsing along Shaanxi North Road from Julu Road south towards Huaihai Road. In addition to Chinese brands and styles are finds from **Nine West**, **Liz Claibourne**, **Clarks** and **Ecco**, along with a number of discount stores.

Sinan Road

The T-junction of Sinan Road and Huaihai Central Road

has developed a strong following among trendy fashion seekers for its international outlets such as **H&M**, **C&A**, **Sephora** and **Zara**. If you mistakenly think you're anywhere but China, visit the bedding store across from H&M for an authentic Chinese retail experience.

Taikang Road

The maze of alleyways around Taikang Road makes for a unique browsing experience. Cafés, art galleries and boutiques in renovated lanehouses sit next to residential homes, giving visitors a

Film and Literature

Unsurprisingly for a city that began over 1500 years ago, Shanghai has rich literary and film traditions. During the city's cultural heyday in the early to mid-20th century, Chinese filmmakers and writers flourished. After the Chinese Civil War, those arts languished for a few years, until a new generation of Chinese directors began to make moody films that explored the complexity and hidden angles of the city, and new writers emerged as well to shine a new light on Shanghai.

Shanghai's Film Industry

Prior to 1949, Shanghai was the centre of Chinese cinema, and the industry was prolific and successful. The most famous personality from that era was **Ruan Lingyu**, a silent-film star who committed suicide at the age of 24. Ruan's most famous film is **Shennu** (Goddess), about a virtuous prostitute, and she is also the subject of a remarkable film by Hong Kong director Stanley Kwan called **The Actress/Centre Stage**.

Films with Ruan and other pre-war Shanghai stars can be seen at the **Old Film Café** in Hongkou (123 Duolun Road; tel: 5696 4763), which screens classic Shanghai films on demand, including some with English subtitles, and has a gallery of photos of 1930s-era stars.

The first Western film shot in Shanghai after the Chinese Civil War was Steven Spielberg's excellent *Empire of the Sun*. Based on a memoir by J.G. Ballard, this gripping film about a teenage boy abandoned in Shanghai during the Japanese occupation is rich

in city scenery. A portion of the film was shot at the 140-year-old Holy Trinity Cathedral, where the young protagonist, played by Christian Bale, went to school. At press time, Holy Trinity Cathedral was set to reopen after a thorough renovation that promised to restore the Gothic red-brick beauty to its pre-war glory (See it at the corner of Jiangxi and Jiujiang roads, in the Bund district; Metro: Line 2, Nanjing East).

The most famous contemporary Shanghai film is a brooding 2000 love story called *Suzhou River*, directed by Shanghai native **Lou Ye**, and starring then-unknown

actress **Zhou Xun**, who is now one of the biggest movie stars in China. Lou went on to further fame with *Purple Butterfly*, a movie about resistance to the Japanese occupation starring Zhang Ziyi.

Literature

Shanghai also has a rich literary tradition, and the figure who towers above all others is the remarkable **Lu Xun**, who focused his sharp pen on the weaknesses and inconsistencies of Chinese society. His most famous work, *The True Story of Ah Q*, is a must-read for anyone interested in Chinese culture, and is a gripping story besides.

However, China's cultural centre of gravity has shifted to Beijing, and much of the country's best fiction is being written by authors from Beijing and elsewhere in China. However, the detective novels of Shanghai native **Qui Xiaolong** are well written and entertaining. They follow the Chinese poetry-loving Detective Chen, who trails his sus-

Left: Danny Boyle at the Shanghai International Film Festival.

Line 1, Shaanxi; Bus: 41, 96, 104; map p.137 E3
A dusty but charming old-style bookstore and coffee shop, with stacks and shelves filled with books old and new, many about China, and all there for the browsing. It also has a good selection of coffee-table books about old Shanghai buildings.

Shanghai Foreign Languages Bookstore
390 Fuzhou Road, near Fujian Road; tel: 6322 3200; 9.30am–7pm; Metro: Line 2, Nanjing East; Bus: 49, 167; map p.134 B3
This six-storey emporium near the Bund is the best bookstore in Shanghai, bursting with books about all things Chinese, including cuisine, language, history, travel, art, crafts, literature and much more. Prices here are a relative bargain.

The most famous Shanghai-related Western movie from the pre-war era is *Shanghai Express*, made in 1932, starring Marlene Dietrich as the good-hearted courtesan Shanghai Lily. Filled with bawdy imagery of old Shanghai, and telling a tender story, it became one of the top-grossing films of its era.

along with a fine selection of books about China, including food, culture, travel and recent fiction. Prices are high, however.

Old China Hand Reading Room
27 Shaoxing Road, near Shaanxi South Road; tel: 6473 2526; daily 10am–midnight; Metro:

pects through gritty Shanghai streets that are rich in urban detail, until he finally gets his man. *Death of a Red Heroine* and *When Red is Black* are two of his best.

Bookstores

Garden Books
325 Chang Le Road, near Shaanxi South Road; tel: 5404 8728; www.gardenbooks.cn; 10am–10pm; Metro: Line 1, Shaanxi; Bus: 26, 146; map p.137 E4
Carries some unique Shanghai books, especially about architecture and history,

Above left: Chines bookstore.
Right: scene from *Bodyguards and Assassins*.

Food and Drink

Food is central to the lives of people in Shanghai, and a night out means a convivial Chinese dinner, sometimes with wine or beer, and always with lively conversation at a round table. But unlike the well-known foods of Guangdong, Beijing and Sichuan, Shanghai cuisine is less famous, although it is becoming more popular. Super-spicy Sichuan is still the city's favourite cuisine, followed by other regional Chinese foods, while in the past 20 years flavours and ingredients and famous chefs have poured in from around the globe, transforming Shanghai into an international food capital much like any other Asian city.

Shanghainese Food

For most of Chinese history, Shanghai was a muddy farming-and-fishing village, while nearby cities like Hangzhou and Nanjing, both former capitals of China, were famous for their beauty, culture, sophistication and fine food. But Shanghai had no great palaces or emperors to inspire its cuisine, so its people turned to the bays and estuaries of the Yangtze delta for their daily meals, and genuine local cuisine still has a heavy reliance on turtles, snails, freshwater crabs and clams, eels, fish, shrimps

and other shallow-water creatures, along with the Chinese staples of chicken and pork, and a rich selection of local vegetables.

Because they had few spices and ingredients, the people of Shanghai relied heavily on soy sauce, oil and sugar for flavour, with most ingredients either stewed or steamed. Vegetable oil was scarce, and to display their wealth, cooks splashed a cup of oil after preparing the food, and the dishes arrived at the table glistening and shiny. Some very authentic Shanghai restaurants still do this.

Even now, Shanghainese food is not especially colour-

ful – it lacks the cheerful rainbow of colour that typifies Cantonese cookery – and often it is dark, fatty, salty, and sweet. The sweet stewed essence and oily abundance make the dishes easier to eat with the daily rice staple.

But modern Shanghai cuisine is starting to change. As the economic epicentre of the country, the city is getting rich and the people are becoming choosier. The food is veering away from its dark and oily origins, and at upscale Shanghai restaurants it is less fatty and less sweet than it once was. Meanwhile, Shanghai is also pulling the more sophisticated cuisine of Hangzhou into its

> Unlike in the West, there is little stigma attached to mild inebriation in Shanghai, and the tipsy gentleman cuts a romantic figure in Chinese history and literature. In modern China as well, the boss is expected to 'let his hair down' at company banquets and dinners. He will offer many toasts, become animated and red-faced and cheerful, and bond with his employees in a way that is not possible in the office.

Left: steamed dumplings.

in the fire. But Beggar's Chicken has since evolved into haute cuisine. In showier restaurants the clay pot is cracked open at the table, but more often the chicken is cooked in a clay shell instead of a pot, and only the lotus leaf is unwrapped at the table. Most restaurants use a tender spring chicken, and stuff it with pork or ham, small dried shrimp, mushrooms, scallions, salt, soy sauce, Shaoxing wine, and sometimes a hint of chilli or black pepper.

Dong Po Rou

This famous marbled pork dish is a classic Shanghai offering. The fat, tender strips of meat are stewed slowly in the classic sauce of soy, sugar and salt until the layers of pork and fat are salty, sweet and tender, and melt in the mouth. It is not health food, but it is tasty, and wholesome during the winter; Chinese diners especially cherish the rich texture.

Longjing Tea Shrimp

This simple but elegant dish hails from Hangzhou, but is now one of the top offerings in the Shanghainese reper-toire. The shrimps are bat-tered and flash fried, then

> Shanghainese diners don't like restaurants that are quiet or empty. A meal out is supposed to be lively and boisterous, or *re nao*, which translates as hot and noisy. The clinking of teacups and plates and glasses, loud rounds of toasting, good-natured banter, shouting wait-resses, playing children and a roomful of happy diners create a *re nao* atmosphere.

orbit, which is lighter, brighter and less sweet, with more of a reliance on freshness and quick cooking.

Famous Dishes

Visitors are encouraged to try any of the following local specialities, which range from simple street food to high-end favourites.

Yellow Croaker

Yellow croaker is one of the signature seafoods of Shanghai. Top restaurants

Left and right: street food ranges from traditional Chinese meat and veg to whole grilled squid.

use wild fish, because farmed croaker can acquire a brackish taste, and a good restaurant will prepare the fish according to its fresh-ness. If fresh, the croaker will be steamed; if less fresh, it will be deep-fried and then braised in a rich sweet sauce heavy on garlic and soy. Deep-fried silky tofu, whole mushrooms and roast garlic cloves often adorn the fish.

Beggar's Chicken

As the tale goes, a beggar stole a chicken, and had nothing to cook it in, so he wrapped it in mud and put it

cooked briefly with longjing tea, which provides a herbal flavour that is lightly sweet, a bit bitter, and very mild. It marries perfectly with the bright, crunchy flavour and texture of the freshwater shrimp, which has a tighter texture and a paler colour than its saltwater cousin.

Dumplings

Shanghai dumplings, or *baozi*, are the city's favourite street food, and every neighbourhood boasts many streetside stands, easily recognised by the cylindrical bamboo steamers, the crowds of people and the fra-

grant puffs of steam. The four main fillings are vegetable *(cai bao)*, pork *(xiao long bao)*, sweet sesame *(zhi ma bao)* and sweet red bean paste *(hong dou bao)*. Eat them in the morning, when they are freshest; most of these hard-working vendors are up at 3am rolling and shaping and steaming their buns for their early customers.

Shanghai Hairy Crab

This unique treat is a cultural phenomenon unlike anything else on earth. Every year from mid-October to the end of December, when the crabs

are ripe with milt or roe, huge crowds of people drive to the shores of nearby **Yangcheng Lake** to eat the hairy crab. The crabs are also available in Shanghai, where they are steamed and served with a sauce of ginger, vinegar and sugar. The interiors are sweet and buttery, with a rich flavour and a superb velvety texture.

Drinks and Desserts

Tea is common with lunch and dinner, and the preferred type in Shanghai is longjing oolong, a mild, semi-fermented tea from Hangzhou that delivers a mild

acidity and subtle flavour, and is a perfect accompaniment to the rich local cuisine.

Beer is cheap and popular, with Tsing Tao, a reliable light pilsner, as the beer of choice. Sometimes, especially at company dinners or banquets, people in Shanghai will drink **huang jiu**, or yellow wine, a sweet, mild wine made from glutinous rice. The best *huang jiu* is *Shaoxing jiu*, a golden amber liquid from a city near Hangzhou, which is made from glutinous rice, millet and ordinary rice, plus water from a famous local lake.

There are no famous Shanghai desserts. As in most parts of China, sliced fruit is served after a meal. One exception is a dish called *ba si*, or candy floss, which is originally from Beijing. At the table, slices of fruit, usually apple or banana, are dipped in melted cane sugar and toasted sesame seeds, and then plunged into a bowl of ice, with the resulting threads resembling fine sugary floss.

Above left: preparing steamed dumplings. **Left:** Shanghai hairy crab. **Above:** a roasted duck stall. **Right:** steamed dumplings with sticky rice.

History

4,000 BC
Prehistoric hunter-gatherers settle in the Yangtze Delta.

1,000 BC
A tiny farming and fishing village is established on the banks of the Huangpu River.

500–1300 AD
Shanghai grows in size and importance, and it develops a trading culture during the Southern Song Dynasty (1127–1279).

1400s
The Huangpu is dredged several times, setting the stage for commercial success.

1554
Shanghai builds a wall to protect itself from Japanese pirates; the circular edges of the wall still define the current borders of Old Town.

1685
The Qing Dynasty opens a Customs Office, and Shanghai grows in commercial importance, with cotton, silk and tea as the key exports.

1839–1845
The British Army invades China, and forces it to sign the Treaty of Nanjing, which gives it a foreign concession in Shanghai. France and America soon establish concessions of their own.

1851–1854
The Taiping Rebellion rages across China, and Chinese residents pour into Shanghai.

1850s
Shanghai's boisterous Golden Age begins, and it becomes one of the fastest-growing and most famous cities on earth. It is rife with crime, but also rich in opportunity for both Chinese and Westerners.

1895
Japan crushes China in a war over the Korean Peninsula, and the Treaty of Shimoneseki is signed, increasing Japanese involvement in Shanghai.

1911
The Qing Dynasty collapses, and a weak and fragmented Nationalist Government takes over the Republic of China.

1921
The Chinese Communist Party is founded in Shanghai; Mao Zedong attends the meeting.

1923
The Hongkong and Shanghai Bank Building opens on the Bund.

1924
Gangster Du Yuesheng takes over the Green Gang, and dominates the city's gambling, opium, prostitution and protection rackets. Du later teams up with Nationalist leader Chiang Kai-shek to purge the city of communists.

1929
The Cathay Hotel, now the Fairmont Peace Hotel, opens on the Bund.

1931–1941
Shanghai becomes a safe haven for Jews fleeing persecution in Europe.

1931–1932
Japan bombs and invades Shanghai, but withdraws under international pressure.

1937
Japan bombs and invades Shanghai again, destroying many buildings and driving many residents out of the city. The Nationalist government retreats to Nanjing.

1945
Japan surrenders, bringing an end to World War 2.

1949
The Communists win the Chinese Civil War and take control of the country. Shanghai's gambling parlours, brothels, and opium dens are shut down. Most foreigners leave, and those that remain are soon expelled.

1958
Mao launches the Great Leap Forward.

1966–1976
The Cultural Revolution paralyzes Shanghai for a decade, before ending with the death of Mao in 1976.

1978
Deng Xiaoping launches the 'openings and reforms' era.

1992
Deng takes his famous 'southern tour' to promote capitalism, and encourages commerce in Shanghai, which he calls the Dragon's Head of the Yangtze Delta.

1994
Former Shanghai mayor Jiang Zemin becomes president of China. Metro Line 1 opens, as does the Oriental Pearl Tower in Pudong.

1998
The Jinmao Tower opens in Pudong.

1999
Pudong International Airport opens, and the city's elevated highway system is finished.

2003
The Maglev train opens in Pudong, and Hu Jintao succeeds Jiang Zemin as president of China.

2004
Shanghai hosts the first-ever Formula One Grand Prix race in China.

2007
Shanghai enjoys its sixth straight year of double-digit economic growth.

2008
The World Financial Centre building opens in Pudong.

2010
Expo 2010 opens in May.

Hotels

Shanghai has surged to the pinnacle of the global hotel scene, as most of the world's finest international hotel chains have hurried to open brand-new flagship properties in this up-and-coming city. They are joined by Asia's top operators of serviced apartment buildings, which offer more space, and kitchens, along with some hotel-style services. Many Chinese operators have pitched in with fine properties of their own, some of them in heritage buildings, or in villa compounds with spacious grounds. Quirky boutique hotels and musty-but-effective government-run hotels round out the spectrum of offerings.

The Bund

Captain Hostel

37 Fuzhou Road; tel: 6323 5053; www.captainhostel.com.cn; $; Metro: Line 2, Nanjing East; Bus: 42, 66, 220; map p.140 B2

This low-budget favourite is cherished for its fine Bund location, just back from the riverfront and a few minutes from Nanjing East Road, and has rooms ranging from quite basic to standard. Even if you don't stay there, the rooftop **Captain's Bar**, with its Pudong views and cheap drinks, is a welcome antidote to the non-stop glitz of its pricey neighbours.

Fairmont Peace Hotel

20 Nanjing Road East, corner Nanjing Road and the Bund; tel: 10 800 714 1088; www. fairmont.com; $$$: Metro: Line 2, Nanjing East; Bus: 55, 910; map p.140 B3

Prices for a standard double room during the peak season:
$ less than US$75
$$ $75–150
$$$ $150–250
$$$$ over $250

The famous old Peace Hotel was still under scaffolding at the time of publication, but Fairmont promises a lavish, top-to-bottom, faithful re-creation of this beloved landmark, which is one of the best-known buildings in China. SEE ALSO ART DECO, P.34

Howard Johnson Plaza

595 Jiu Jiang Road; tel: 3313 4888; www.hojochina.com; $$$ Metro: Lines 1, 2, People's Square; Bus: 37, 167, 14; map p.134 A3

The manager calls this a 4.75-star hotel, and the description fits perfectly. The Howard Johnson fills a key niche: a sort-of-new international-standard hotel that effortlessly delivers all the key amenities, including an excellent Cantonese restaurant, at a reasonable price, and with a fine location overlooking Nanjing East pedestrian road.

Langham Yangtze Boutique

740 Hankou Road; tel: 6080 0800; www.langhamhotels.com; $$$$; Metro: Lines 1, 2, People's Square; map p.134 A3

Shanghai is one of the best cities in Asia to rent a **serviced apartment** instead of a hotel room. Serviced apartments offer many of the amenities of a full-service hotel, such as daily room cleaning, fitness centre and pool, and a restaurant, and they also provide bigger rooms, more space and a fully equipped kitchen. Given the fierce competition in Shanghai, most are very willing to book guests for one or two nights, but the rates drop with stays of a week or more.

So this is what the gilded age looked like: the Langham Yangtze is located in a 1934 Art Deco-hybrid building, and the pocket-sized hotel reopened in 2009 with gorgeous Art Deco-inspired interiors, including the stacked geometrical shapes, bold lines and chrome fittings of the era. Some of the rooms have balconies, and all of them feature bold 1930s-style designs coupled with soft, padded luxury.

Le Royal Méridien

789 Nanjing Road East; tel: 3318 9999; www.starwood; $$$$;

Left: Le Royal Méridien.

with a Chinese pagoda roof, and offers a wide range of rooms, from hostel-style dorm rooms (US$15 per night) up to suites ($100 per night).

People's Park Area

Citadines Shanghai Jinqiao serviced apartment
55 Beijing Road West; tel: 2308 6666; www.citadines.com/en/china/shanghai/jinqiao/location.html; $$; Metro: line 2, Jinan Temple, then taxi; Bus: 93, 921; map p.132 B1
Citadines is the least expensive of the three serviced apartment brands offered by Singapore-based Ascott International, yet is perfectly adequate, especially for long-stay visitors on a budget. This property has comfortable rooms ranging from studios to two-bedrooms, with all the modern amenities and fully equipped kitchens.

JW Marriott Hotel

399 Nanjing Road West; tel: 5359 4969; www.marriotthotels.com/shajw; $$$$; Metro: Lines 1, 2, People's Square; map p.133 E2
JW Marriott Shanghai Tomorrow Square is a hotel-in-a-tower, with a functional

Metro: Lines 1, 2, People's Square; map p.134 A3
At the top of the Shimao Plaza, this 333m (1,092ft) 60-storey tower filled with sheared glass and sharp angles opened in 2005 at the corner of People's Park and Nanjing East Road. The interiors are filled with artwork, and the bars and restaurants are shaped by the exterior angles of the building, which give it a unique interior ambience.

Peninsula Shanghai

32 Zhongshan Dong Yi Road; tel: 2327 2888; www.peninsula.com; $$$$; Bus: 37, 55, 65; map p.140 B4
The long-awaited opening of the Peninsula, in a prime property near Suzhou Creek on the Bund, had yet to occur at the time of publishing.

Westin Bund Centre

88 Central Henan Road; tel: 6335 1888; www.starwood.com; $$$$; Bus: 66, 71, 929; map p.140 A1
Its readily recognisable pineapple-shaped crown is visible from as far away as Pudong, and the hotel is equally well known for its

landmark Sunday brunch, which features food choices from every hemisphere, spiced up with Chinese dancers, acrobats and jugglers. The Westin's 'heavenly beds' are still the most comfortable sleeping setups in town.

Old Town

Oriental Bund Hotel (formerly the Xing Yu Hotel)
386 Ren Min Road; tel: 6333 8888; $$; Metro: Line 8, Dashijie; map p.135 C2
Another relatively new mid-level hotel that is giving the government-managed properties a run for their money, the entirely adequate Oriental Bund has comfortable rooms, a small gym, a cosy business centre and a fine location not far from Yuyuan Garden.

YMCA Hotel

123 Xi Zang Road South; tel: 6326 1040; www.ymcahotel.com/english/index.htm; $; Metro: Line 1, Huangpi; map p.134 B2
The Jinjiang YMCA is in a 1929 classical-style building

Right: Westin Bund Centre.

street-level entrance and an elegant main lobby on the 38th floor. The rooms feature silk textured wallpaper, mahogany tea chests, and marble tubs that complement business-oriented amenities like laptop-sized room safes and multiple telephones. Don't miss **JW's Lounge**, perched on the 40th floor, which has a 50-Martini menu and fine views of the city. SEE ALSO ARCHITECTURE, P.31

Pacific Hotel

108 Nanjing Road West; tel: 6327 6226; www.pacific. jinjianghotels.com; $$; Metro: Lines 1, 2, People's Square; map p.134 A3

Another ageing beauty on People's Park, with a classical design capped by an iconic golden-domed clock tower, the Pacific has suffered a similar fate as the Park *(see below)*. Be sure to ask for a room with a balcony.

Park Hotel

170 Nanjing Road West; tel: 6327 5225; www.parkhotel.com.cn; $$; Metro: Lines 1, 2, People's Square; map p.134 A3

Formerly the tallest building in Asia and the finest hotel in the hemisphere, the venerable old Park, designed by famous architect László Hudec, has slipped into a regrettable state of faded glory. Nonetheless, its lobby, rooms and restaurants, while awaiting the sort of loving, top-to-bottom renovation enjoyed by the Peace Hotel, still manage to evoke the ambience of a bygone era, and are perfect for nostalgia seekers. SEE ALSO ART DECO, P.35

Radisson Hotel Shanghai New World

88 Nanjing Road West; tel: 6359 9999; www.radisson.com/ shanghaicn_newworld; $$; Metro: Lines 1, 2, People's Square; map p.134 A3

The 'flying saucer' cap of the Radisson's revolving restaurant is a modern icon that hovers over People's Park, and beneath that flying saucer are 520 very comfortable rooms. On the cutting edge a couple of decades ago, the building has aged gracefully, and now has that dated-but-charming look. Ditto for the Radisson itself, a comfortable, well-run property known for its good location and fine views of the city.

Xintiandi Area

88 Xintiandi

380 Huang Pi Road South; tel: 5383 8833; www.88xintiandi. com; $$$$; Metro: Line 1, Huangpi; map p.138 A4

This beautiful new property in the heart of Xintiandi has quickly established itself as one of the classiest addresses in town. A refreshing departure from the chain hotels, it has a wide selection of one- and two-bedroom suites, post-modern electronics and other cutting-edge decor combined with old world polished-wood and brass-rail touches. Try to get a room with a balcony.

Fraser Residence Shanghai

98 Shou Ning Road; tel: 2308 0000; shanghai.frasers hospitality.com; $$–$$$; Metro: Line 8, Dashijie; Bus: 17, 23, 42; map p.134 B1

An unexpected treat in a sur-

prising and very convenient location, Fraser Residence has large, well-appointed one- and two-bedroom units, a thoughtful array of kitchen equipment, a swimming pool, and a restaurant that is a firm local favourite: David Laris's **Fat Olive**.

SEE ALSO RESTAURANTS, P.103

Lapis Casa

68 Taicang Road; tel: 5382 1600; www.lapiscasahotel.com; $$$; Metro: Line 1, Huangpi; map p.134 A1

This cosy 18-room mini-boutique hotel, once a Forestry Bureau building, has a classy courtyard and a pocket-sized lobby filled with antiques. In the halls and stairwells, stained-glass windows send shafts of multi-coloured light dancing into the corridors, while Mediterranean touches are evident in the arched doorways and tile floors. Inside the rooms, plush velvet curtains add a touch of glamour, while the four-poster canopy beds, elegant desk-and-lamp combos, marble basins and claw-foot bathtubs evoke concession-

era opulence, albeit coupled with wireless Internet, plasma TV and a free minibar.

Shama Luxe at Xintiandi

168 Shun Chang Road; tel: 2320 6688; www.shama.com; $$–$$$; Metro: Line 1, Xujiahui; map p.138 A4

Shama Luxe at Xintiandi has 100 one-, two- and three-bedroom units in styles ranging from traditional to ultra-modern pads spangled in geometrical patterns of red, grey, white and black. Regardless of style, all rooms have fully equipped kitchens, and the property has a gym, spa, swimming pool and other hotel-style features.

Hongkou and Suzhou Creek

Broadway Mansions

20 Suzhou Road North; tel: 6324

> A battle is raging for your accommodation dollar in Shanghai, and bargains abound. In the run-up to Expo 2010, hotels and serviced apartments poured into the city to open new properties, creating a remarkable surplus of rooms. But what is challenging for hotels is good for visitors, so be sure to ask for a good rate.

6260; www.broadwaymansions. com; $$; Bus: 25, 868; map p.134 C4

A historic old gem that was built in 1934 and later served as the home of the Shanghai Foreign Correspondents' Club, the huge symmetrical Art Deco Broadway Mansions faces the Bund to the north, and is one of the city's most prominent landmarks. It has some modern touches, such as remodelled rooms and Internet access, but stay here for the views and the history. Rooms with river views are more costly, but might be worth it; there is no view on earth like the Huangpu River at night.

Hyatt on the Bund

199 Huangpu Road; tel: 6393 1234; www.shanghai.bund.hyatt. com/hyatt/hotels; $$$; Metro: Line 2, Nanjing East, then taxi; Bus: 33, 37, 921; map p.135 C4

When it opened this riverfront property became the first five-star hotel in Hongkou, just north of the Bund. A 631-room giant, it has two wings connected by a glass lobby, quiet padded hallways that ooze class, and outside elevators that whisk guests high up into the Shanghai sky. The twin towers are set at angles

Left: Pujiang Hotel *(see p.72)*.
Above: Four Seasons Hotel *(see p.72)*.

71

Prices for a standard double
room during the peak season:
$ less than US$75
$$ $75–150
$$$ $150–250
$$$$ over $250

to the Huangpu River, a setup
that provides every room
above the 11th floor with
either a bird's-eye view of the
iconic Bund, or a wonderful
view of brand-new Pudong.

Motel 168

300 Huoshan Road; tel: 5117
1111; www.motel168.com; $;
Metro: Line 4, Dalian
One of about 70 Motel 168s
in Shanghai, it delivers everything the budget traveller
could want: bright, clean
rooms, a business centre and
free broadband, along with a
reliable online reservations
system – although only in
Chinese – and a bit of
spoken English.

Pujiang Hotel, also called
Astor House

15 Huangpu Road; tel: 6324
6388; www.pujianghotel.com;
$$; Metro: Line 2, Nanjing East,
then 5-minute taxi; Bus: 868;
map p.135 C4
Albert Einstein, Ulysses S.
Grant, Bertrand Russell and

Charlie Chaplin stayed in the
Astor House, and it was
home to the first electric
lights ever used in China.
This atmospheric old building
is ripe for a revamp, but stay
there before that happens,
because for now, the old
Pujiang is a wonderful old
gem that is still in a very
authentic state.
SEE ALSO ARCHITECTURE, P.29

Nanjing Road West Area
Four Seasons Shanghai

500 Weihai Road; tel: 6256
8888; www.fourseasons.
com/shanghai; $$$; Metro:
Line 2, Nanjing West; map
p.133 D2
With a location that is reasonably close to People's
Park, while also straddling
the city's two best shopping
thoroughfares – Nanjing
Road West and Huaihai Road
Central – the five-star Four
Seasons is a good choice for
those who have some extra
money to spend. And don't
tell anyone, but it is the top
choice of hotel professionals
when they travel at their own
expense.

JC Mandarin

1225 Nanjing Road West; tel:
6279 1888; www.jcmandarin.
com; $$; Metro: Line 2, between

Jinan Temple and Nanjing West;
map p.133 C2
An older but still comfortable
four-star property with a great
location in the heart of the
city's priciest shopping dis-
trict, and just a stone's throw
away from the Shanghai Exhi-
bition Centre. That enormous
hand-painted lacquer mural in
the lobby is Admiral Zheng
He, a Chinese maritime
explorer of the early 1400s.

JIA Shanghai

931 Nanjing Road West; tel: 6217
9000; www.jiashanghai. com;
$$$; Metro: Line 2, Nanjing West;
map p.133 D2
A quirky little hotel in a
1920s-era building, JIA
Shanghai is filled with playful
design details in bright primary colours. The lobby is
lean and spare, with an open
layout, and is sprinkled with
black and red modern eclec-
tia – think wire-frame bicycles
and paired panda bears. The
55 rooms are similarly eclectic, with polished black counters, green ottomans, and
snow-white beds with
mustard-yellow duvets. They
also feature cosy kitch-
enettes, because after all, *jia*
means 'home' in Chinese.

Portman Ritz-Carlton

1376 Nanjing Road West; tel:
6279 8888; www.ritz-carlton.
com; $$$$; Metro: Line 2,
between Jinan Temple and
Nanjing West; map p.133 C2
Located in the iconic Shanghai Centre, this is without
doubt the most famous hotel
in Shanghai, and the prestige
of the address is beyond
doubt. The Portman com-
bines smooth luxury with a
bustling location in the Jing
An district, surrounded by a
wealth of sightseeing and
dining choices, and the complex as a whole is an architectural treasure.

PuLi Hotel and Spa

1 Changde Road; pre-opening tel: 3203 9999; www.thepuli. com; $$$$; Metro: Line 2, Jinan Temple; map p.132 C1

This touch of Southeast Asian spa culture, albeit set in the heart of Shanghai, opened in late 2009, introducing the city to an urban resort filled with trickling water, spa treatments, park views and stratospheric thread counts.

Shanghai Centre

1376 Nanjing Road West; tel: 6279 8600; www.shanghai centre.com; $$–$$$$; Metro: Line 2, between Jinan Temple and Nanjing West; map p.133 C2

An excellent and little-known accommodation option, and a genuine bargain, this serviced apartment offers daily stays in a variety of rooms, from studios to three-bedroom suites.

Swissôtel Grand Shanghai

1 Yu Yuan Road; tel: 5355 9898; www.swissotel.com/shanghai; $$$; Metro: Line 2, Jinan Temple; map p.132 C1

Another new arrival in the accommodation market, the Swissôtel opened in 2008 in the fast-changing neighbourhood just north of Nanjing Road. Its key design feature is a grand lobby of polished marble and vaulting gold ceilings, punctuated by a sweeping central staircase.

Urbn Hotel

183 Jiao Zhou Street; tel: 5153 4600; www.urbnhotels.com; $$$; Metro: Line 2, Jinan Temple; map p.132 B2

China's first carbon-neutral hotel is far more environ-

mentally friendly than the former factory that it replaced, and it has rapidly assumed a status as one of the city's most talked-about hotels. Design-wise, the little boutique property is an effortless success that is smooth and compelling, without trying too hard.

Former French Concession North

Hengshan Moller Villa

30 Shaanxi Road South; tel: 6247 8881; www.moller villa.com; $$; Metro: Line 2, Nanjing West, then taxi; Bus: 24; map p.136 B1

This former fantasy-castle home was converted to a hotel in 2001, and we can all be thankful for that, because now it is possible to walk in, or book a room, and have a first-hand look at the interiors of a truly remarkable building. For greater ambience, although perhaps not greater comfort, book a room in the old building, not the annexe.

SEE ALSO ARCHITECTURE, P.30, 31

Hilton Hotel

250 Huashan Road; tel: 6248 0000; www.hilton.com; $$$; Metro: Line 2, Jinan Temple;

> The **peak season** for hotels in Shanghai is September, October, November and early December, when they fill up with business travellers and with sightseers enjoying the milder weather. Spring is the second high season, although not as busy as the autumn, while winters and summers are traditionally low travel seasons when good rates are plentiful. And because business travellers prefer to stay during weekdays, many hotels offer good rates, or enticing extras, on Saturdays.

Left: Swissôtel. **Above:** Hengshan Moller Villa.

map p.136 B4

A venerable hotel that has established itself as an accommodation landmark, the Hilton staked out its turf in an old Concession location several decades ago, where an entire cottage industry of bars and restaurants has established itself in the early days of five-star hotels in Shanghai. Don't miss the very elaborate toy train set that chugs around the lobby during the holidays.

Jing An Hotel

370 Huashan Road; tel: 6248 1888; $$; Metro: Line 2, Jinan Temple; map p.136 B4

A hotel that will appeal to Shanghai history buffs, the Jing An is in a 1935 building of Spanish-style design, surrounded by vast colonial-era lawns and trees. Its rooms have high ceilings, crown mouldings, wood panels and graceful arched designs.

Jinjiang Hotel

59 Maoming Road South; tel: 6258 2582; www.jinjiang hotels.com; $$; Metro: Line 1, Shaanxi; map p.133 D1

The Jinjiang has two wings, both with impressive pedigrees: the Cathay Building is a

Gothic-style structure, while the Grosvenor House is impressively large, coffee-brown Art Deco giant. Rooms in both wings feature the high ceilings of the gilded age, but the history trumps the rooms: Richard Nixon and Mao Zedong signed the Shanghai Communiqué here in 1972.

Jinjiang Tower

161 Changle Road; tel: 6415 1188; www.jinjianghotels.com; $$; Metro: Line 1, Shaanxi; map p.133 E1

With its revolving 41st-floor restaurant lording it over the comparatively low-rise streets of the old French Concession, Jinjiang Tower is a hard-to-miss neighbourhood landmark. It is relatively newer than most Jinjiang Group hotels, and the facilities and service are good, but its chief virtue, besides the views, is a plum Huaihai Road location.

Mansion Hotel

82 Xinle Road; tel: 5403 9888; www.chinamansionhotel.com; $$$$; Metro: Line 1, Shaanxi; map p.137 D4

The Mansion is a grand hotel in miniature, small in stature but large in palatial trappings

and old-world charm. The 1920s-era building has just 30 rooms, but its garden courtyard, high-ceilinged lobby and dressy doormen evoke images of classic grandeur, while the rooms feature carpeted wood floors, antique mirrors and chandeliered ceilings, along with modern touches like triple-glazed windows.

Okura Garden Hotel

58 Maoming Road South; tel: 6415 1111; www.gardenhotel shanghai.com; Metro: line 1, Shanxi Station; map p.133 D1

An old-meets-new property managed by Japan's Okura group, featuring a modern high-rise tower perched adjacent to a historic base: the public areas of the hotel occupy the renovated Cercle Sportif Français (French Club), with many of the historic details and sprawling gardens still intact.

Old House Inn

No. 16, Lane 351, Huashan Road; tel: 6249 6118; www.old house.cn; $; Metro: Line 2, Jinan Temple, then taxi; map p.136 B4

A charming guesthouse-style boutique hotel in an old lane-house on the edge of the

Left: Crowne `Plaza Shanghai.

Concession area. With just 12 rooms, all in traditional Chinese decor, this is a genuine old-school retreat from the packed streets of the city.

Taiyuan Villa
160 Taiyuan Road; tel: 6471 6688; www.ruijinhotelsh.com; $$; Metro: Line 1, Hengshan, then taxi; map p.137 C2
One of the nicest mansions in the French Concession and dating back to the 1920s, Taiyuan Villa was once the home of General George Marshall, as well as Mao's dragon-lady fourth wife, Jiang Qing (though not at the same time). Refurbished using 1930s-style Shanghai furniture, the rooms overlook the villa's sprawling lawns.

Former French Concession South
Hengshan Picardie Hotel
534 Hengshan Road; tel: 6437 2929; www.hengshanhotel.com; $$; Metro: line 1, Hengshan Station; map p.136 B1
Built in 1936 as the Picardie Apartments, it has an imposing ochre-yellow exterior, yet it is one of the plainest Art Deco buildings in Shanghai, and lost much of its historic charm after a 2002 refurbishment that modernised the rooms and added an ornate, gilded touch to public areas. It does have fine views of Xujiahui Park, and convenient access to the Hengshan Road bar area.

Regal International East Asia Hotel
516 Hengshan Road; tel: 6415 5588; www.regal-eastasia.com; Metro: Line 1, Hengshan; map p.136 B1
A slick, modern five-star located in the diplomatic district, just outside the bustling new hub of Xujiahui and a

five-minute drive from Central Huaihai Road. Hengshan Park and Xujiahui Park are across the street, and the Xujiahui shopping and business district is a five-minute walk. This would be a good choice for partiers, as the Hengshan Road bar-and-restaurant strip is just steps away.

Ruijin Guesthouse
118 Ruijin No. 2 Road; tel: 6472 5222; www.ruijinhotelsh.com; $$; Metro: Line 1, Shaanxi; map p.137 E3
Five renovated historic villas, all with different prices, are set in an expansive estate dotted with fountains and pavilions, and located in the heart of the old French Concession.

Somerset Xu Hui
888 Shanxi Road South; tel: 6466 0888; www.somerset.com/index.html?; $$; Metro: Line 1, Shaanxi, then taxi; map p.137 D2
At around US$80 per night for a one-bedroom apartment with a kitchen in the Ascott Group's mid-market brand, this qualifies as a genuine accommodation bargain. The location is not bad either, on Shanxi Road South, at the southern fringe of the old French Concession.

Two mainland Chinese groups own and operate most of the city's heritage hotels. Hengshan Hotels and Resorts operates Broadway Mansions, Hengshan Picardie Hotel, Hengshan Moller Villa and the Astor House, and formerly the Yangtze hotel, before the Langham group took it over in 2009. The Jinjiang Group has in its portfolio the Park, the Pacific, the Jinjiang and the Metropole, and formerly operated the Peace Hotel, before Fairmont began to manage it.

Prices for a standard double room during the peak season:
$ less than US$75
$$ $75–150
$$$ $150–250
$$$$ over $250

Western Shanghai
Crowne Plaza Shanghai
400 Pan Yu Road; tel: 6145 8888; www.ichotelsgroup.com; $$; Metro: Line 2, Jiangsu, then taxi; Bus: 76, 946; map p.136 A3
A well-run four-star that straddles the western edge of the old Concession, and soon to be served when Metro Line 10 opens, Crowne Plaza Shanghai is a good choice for anyone doing business – or visiting friends or relatives – in the sprawling western suburbs.

Hua Ting Hotel and Towers
1200 Cao Xi Road North; tel: 6439 1000; www.huatinghotel-shanghai.com; $$; Metro: Lines 1, 4, Shanghai Indoor Stadium
Formerly the Sheraton, this 780-room giant was the city's first-ever international hotel, and Xujiahui district has grown up around it, enclosing it in an ever-busier network of elevated highways and busy roads, while Shanghai Stadium is just across the street. There are some faint echoes of its former glory, including the lobby, and it has an excellent Cantonese restaurant.

Radisson Plaza Xingguo Hotel
78 Xingguo Road; tel: 6212 9998; www.radisson.com; $$; Metro: Line 2, Jiangsu, then taxi; Bus: 96, 113, 506
This contemporary high-rise sits at the edge of the former Butterfield and Swire compound and is closer to the French Concession area than it is to the city's far west. On its 6 hectares (15 acres) of

lawn are several old villas (only open to state visitors and long-term guests), including the historic Building Number One, where Mao Zedong stayed when he was in town. Excellent facilities with tastefully furnished and generous-sized rooms.

Renaissance Yangtze
2099 Yan An Road West; tel: 6275 0000; www.marriott.com; $$$; Metro: Line 2, Loushanguan, then taxi; Bus: 507, 709, 749

This hotel's great asset is its location in the midst of all the convention centres of western Shanghai, including the giant Shanghai Mart. It is conveniently located on the Yan'An expressway, which whisks visitors to the Bund, or, in the other direction, to Hongqiao Airport.

Shama Luxe Huashan
211 Xing Fu Road; tel: 2211 9288; www.shama.com; $$–$$$$; Bus: 44, 113, 506

This serviced apartment sits in a vertical slice of building in one of the quieter parts of the old French Concession. Its rooms are bigger than the usual serviced apartment offerings, and it offers three- and four-bedroom units. The chain's 'no boundaries' lifestyle programme offers guests access to a variety of private clubs, along with discounts at shops and restaurants, and is a good entrée into the city for newcomers.

Shama Xujiahui
Lane 81, Xin Geng Road; tel: 2411 8888; www.shama.com; $$–$$$; Metro: Line 1, Xujiahui; Bus: 15, 44, 72

The one- to three-bedroom units at Shama Xujiahui are surrounded by the non-stop throb of Xujiahui, one of the city's busiest districts, while the units themselves feature smooth, contemporary designs and chic simplicity.

Sheraton Hongqiao
5 Zunyi Road South; tel: 6275 8888; www.starwood.com; $$$; Metro: Line 2, Loushanguan, then taxi

The former Sheraton Grand Taipingyang has been re-branded for a second time, but the four-star flair and reliable service are still here. A business traveller's favourite, it is close to the Shanghai Everbright Convention and Exhibition Centre, and at night, it boasts the Sheraton Sweet Sleeper, a soft white world of feather pillows and high thread counts. Its deli is by far the best in town, and attracts people from downtown Shanghai, about 8km (5 miles) away.

Xijiao State Guesthouse
1921 Hongqiao Road; tel: 6219 8800; www.hotelxijiao.com; $$$; Metro: Line 2, Loushanguan, then taxi; Bus: 519, 748, 757

What sets this place apart is its picturesque setting in an 80-hectare (200-acre) woodland park. Extensively refurbished in 2005, it has stylish rooms as well as villas, though the latter are for long-term guests and are scattered throughout the beautiful grounds among flowers and trees. Convenient for business in the Hongqiao area, but it is a 20-minute drive from the city centre.

Pudong

Courtyard by Marriott
838 Dongfang Road; tel: 6886 7886; www.marriott.com; $$; Metro: Line 2, Century Avenue

Comfortable hotel geared for the business traveller with an eye on the balance sheet. Rooms have generously sized work desks, two phones with dataports, and the full range of business amenities, including meeting facilities. Located near Lujiazui, across the street from the St Regis.

Fraser Suites Top Glory Shanghai
No. 1, Lane 600, Yincheng Road Central; tel: 6378 8888; www.shanghai-suites.frasers hospitality.com; $$$$; Metro: Line 2, Lujiazui

Opened in late 2008, Fraser Suites has big two- and three-bedroom units decorated in modern suburban style, with balconies and picture-window views of the adjacent Huangpu River. It is near Riverfront Park and close to the financial district of Lujiazui, and is right across from the fast-rising Shanghai

Tower. Amenities include a lagoon-like outdoor swimming pool, daily room cleaning and well-equipped kitchens.

Grand Hyatt Shanghai
88 Century Avenue, Jinmao Tower; tel: 5049 1234; www. shanghai.grand.hyatt.com $$$$; Metro: Line 2, Dongchang; map p.135 E3

Some of its thunder was stolen by the Park Hyatt, which hovers high above the Grand Hyatt just 50m/yds away, but the Grand has an air of quiet class and graceful efficiency that comes with experience. As the world's second-tallest hotel, it has tremendous city views, especially from the lobby and from the **Cloud Nine** bar, and its eye-catching interior canyon is a design hallmark for the ages.
SEE ALSO BARS AND CAFÉS, P.43

InterContinental Pudong
777 Zhangyang Road; tel: 5835 6666; www.ichotelsgroup.com/ intercontinental/en/gb/locations/ shanghai; $$$; Metro: Lines 4, 6, Dongfang; Bus: 82, 130, 338

The InterCon was renovated in 2009, and it shows, as the public areas and 308 guest-rooms have emerged sparkling from the recent revamp. It has a good location, a few blocks from Lujiazui, the heart of downtown Pudong.

Novotel Atlantis Shanghai
728 Pudong Avenue; tel: 5036 6666; www.accorhotels-asia.com; $$; Metro: Line 4, Pudong Avenue

The city's most elegant four-star hotel is very good value for money, and offers easy access to the more distant attractions of Pudong. The rooms are smallish, but that

only makes its European sense of style all the more genuine. Restaurants include the revolving **ART50** restaurant, which has eye-catching art exhibits to accompany the eye-watering views.

Park Hyatt Shanghai
100 Century Avenue; tel: 6888 1234; http://shanghai.park.hyatt. com; $$$$; Metro: Line 2, Dongchang

This monumental property, beautiful beyond description, it is a gilded icon to the city's new golden age, a richly textured chrome-and-glass fantasy palace filled with floor-to-ceiling windows, soaring interior canyons, spacious imposing chambers, a must-see infinity swimming pool, and many other delicious spaces that surprise and delight. And don't forget the views – this is the world's tallest hotel, and you never forget it.

Pudong Shangri-La
33 Fucheng Road; tel: 6882 6888; www.shangri-la.com; $$$$; Metro: Line 2, Lujiazui

A fine five-star with a superb location, the Shangri-La is a tale of two towers: the older wing near the river is rather uneasily joined to the new 36-storey tower via a long annexe. Expect spacious rooms, first-class service, good views, and some of the best dining in the city, along with a superior on-site spa. Hint: try the Himalayan Bath.

Ramada Pudong Airport
1100 Qi Hang Road; tel: 3849 4949; www.ramadaairportpd. com; $$; Bus: Airport Bus No. 8

Close to the gateway Pudong Airport, this hotel is a boon for travellers with tight flight connections. There is a full range of restaurants and a health club, and all the TVs receive instant flight informa-

tion. And don't worry about all those roaring jets – the windows are double-glazed.

St Regis
889 Dong Fang Road; tel: 5050 4567; www.starwood.com/ stregis; $$$$; Metro: Line 2, Dongfang

The jewel of Dong Fang Road, the St Regis is epitome of understated luxury. Among the many highlights of this property at the eastern end of the Century Boulevard strip are the 24-hour butler, ergonomic office chairs, and **Danieli's**, a superior Italian restaurant.

Prices for a standard double room during the peak season:
$ less than US$75
$$ $75–150
$$$ $150–250
$$$$ over $250

Left: InterContinental Pudong. **Right:** St Regis.

Infrastructure

Shanghai is experiencing astounding infrastructure growth, as cloud-piercing office towers, lavish new five-star hotels and shiny new shopping malls are springing up like bamboo shoots after a spring rain. But not all the building is private: the Shanghai government is keeping pace with a series of dramatic public works. New subway lines, bridges, tunnels, a cruise-ship dock, airport runways and terminals, highways, parks, a World Expo – you name it, and Shanghai is building it. The city has no shortage of bold plans, and no shortage of money – up to US$45 billion, by some estimates – to accomplish those plans.

Shanghai Metro

Most of the ongoing public works projects are designed to ease transport bottlenecks. Among the most impressive is the Shanghai Metro, where new lines and new stations seem to open up every month or two. Using a new tunnelling technology that doesn't require digging up the streets, Shanghai has quietly added an astounding amount of subway track: from 2005 to 2009, seven brand-new Metro lines were opened, giving the city a total of nine, and adding nearly 250km (155 miles) of new track and almost 200 stations. And the system is still growing: by 2020, Shanghai Metro will have 20 lines and 900km (560 miles) of track.
SEE ALSO TRANSPORT, P.124

Maglev

Another plan will extend the Maglev (magnetic levitation) train from its current stop in the hinterlands of Pudong to the Expo 2010 site, and from there to the Hongqiao domestic airport. That will

cut the travel time between the airports from about an hour and a half, depending upon traffic, to just 15 minutes. Meanwhile a second line, still in the planning stages at the time of publication, will branch off from the first and connect to Hangzhou, 145km (90 miles) away.

A couple of high-powered airport projects are also under way. A new passenger terminal opened at the Pudong International Airport in 2007, but a third terminal and three new runways are planned. When completed, Shanghai will have more passenger capacity than Beijing and Guangzhou combined. Hongqiao Airport, which

serves mostly domestic flights, is also gaining a much-needed new terminal and a second runway.

Cruise Terminal

One of the sexiest projects is the new cruise-ship terminal, because it is in downtown Shanghai, on the North Bund

One of the jokes about Shanghai goes like this: it will be a great place if they ever finish it. And while the construction sometimes seems ubiquitous, they do plan to finish it. The deadline is 1 May 2010, when World Expo 2010 opens, and most major projects are targeted for completion before that date.

Left: China Pavilion for World Expo 2010.

Zhongshan East Road Number 1, the busy highway that divided the Bund buildings from the waterfront promenade. With the street traffic much reduced, the rest of the Bund was converted into a broad and user-friendly promenade that sports a brand-new dock to serve the ever-increasing fleet of sightseeing boats on the Huangpu River.

Expo Cleaning

Not all the projects are dramatic: Shanghai has also rolled up its sleeves and concentrated on smaller street-level neighbourhood improvements that tourists will notice as well. In the two years leading up to the Expo, most of the city sidewalks were replaced and the streets re-paved, and almost every building in town was given a facelift and a paint job, all in preparation for the most ambitious plan of all, the US$4.6 billion World Expo 2010.

SEE ALSO EXPO 2010, P.54–5

Three dramatic **bridges** connect Shanghai proper to Pudong: the Yangpu, Nanpu and Lupu bridges. The Lupu is the world's longest arch bridge, while the Yangpu is one of the world's longest cable-stayed suspension bridge. But from now on, the government has declared, only tunnels will be allowed to connect Pudong with Puxi in downtown Shanghai, and no new bridges will be constructed in the city core, although they are still going up in the suburbs.

ished, it will be able to dock four mammoth cruise ships at a time.

The New Bund

Not all of the building projects are transport related. The most eagerly anticipated of all, perhaps, was the Bund renovation. In the year preceding Expo 2010, the Bund became a vast and busy building site, during which a tunnel was built beneath

waterfront near Suzhou Creek. The first phase of the project opened in 2009, and immediately the world's top cruise lines began sailing to the new dock, setting the stage for further growth: three more berths are under way, along with a 3.66-sq-km (1.44-sq-mile) complex that will contain a hotel, shopping malls and other tourist-friendly amenities. When fin-

Left and right: construction is frenetic: the deadline is 1 May 2010.

Language

Mandarin is China's official language. In addition to Mandarin, known as *putonghua*, most Chinese speak local dialects. In Shanghai, the dialect is Shanghainese, or *Shanghaihua*. Written Chinese uses characters based on pictograms, which are pictorial representations of ideas. The standard romanisation system for Chinese characters is known as *hanyu pinyin*. It has been in use since 1958, and is used throughout this book. Some 6,000–8,000 characters are in regular use; 3,000 are sufficient for reading a newspaper. In mainland China, simplified characters are used, while Hong Kong and Taiwan use more complex characters.

Basic Rules

Tones make it difficult for foreigners to speak Mandarin, as different tones give the same syllable completely different meanings. Take the four tones of the syllable *ma* for instance: the first tone *mā* means 'mother'; the second tone *má* means 'hemp'; the third tone *mǎ* means 'horse'; and the fourth tone *mà* means 'to scold'. There is also a fifth, 'neutral' tone. There is a standard set of diacritical marks to indicate tones:
mā = high and even tone
má = rising tone
mǎ = falling then rising tone
mà = falling tone

Pronunciation

The pronunciation of consonants in hanyu pinyin is similar to those in English. The i after the consonants ch, c, r, sh, s, z, zh is not pronounced; it indicates that the preceding sound is lengthened.

Greetings

Hello *Nǐ hǎo* 你好
How are you? *Nǐ hǎo ma?* 你好吗?

Thank you *Xièxie* 谢谢
Goodbye *Zài jiàn* 再见
My name is… *Wǒ jiào…* 我叫…
What is your name? *Nín jiào shénme míngzi?* 您叫什么名字?
I am very happy… *Wǒ hěn gāoxìng…* 我很高兴…
Can you speak English? *Nín huì shuō Yīngyǔ ma?* 您会说英语吗?
Can you speak Chinese? *Nín huì shuō Hànyǔ ma?* 您会说汉语吗?
I cannot speak Chinese *Wǒ bù huì hànyǔ* 我不会汉语
I do not understand *Wǒ bù dǒng* 我不懂
Do you understand? *Nín dǒng ma?* 您懂吗?
Please speak a little slower *Qǐng nín shuō màn yìdiǎn* 请您说慢一点
What is this called? *Zhège jiào shénme?* 这个叫什么?
How do you say… *…Zěnme shuō?* …怎么说?
Please *Qǐng* 请
Sorry *Duìbuqǐ* 对不起

Pronouns

My/mine *Wǒ/wǒde* 我/我的
You/yours (singular) *Nǐ/nǐde* 你/你的

He/his/she/hers *Tā/tāde/tā/tāde* 他/他的/她/她的
We/ours *Wǒmen/wǒmende* 我们/我们的
They/theirs *Tāmen/tāmende* 他们/他们的

Travel

Where is it? *Zài nǎr?* …在哪儿?
Do you have it here? *Zhèr… yǒu ma?* 这儿有…吗?
No/it's not here/there aren't any *Méi yǒu* 没有
Hotel *Fàndiàn/bīnguǎn* 饭店/宾馆
Restaurant *Fànguǎn* 饭馆
Bank *Yínháng* 银行
Post office *Yóujú* 邮局
Toilet *Cèsuǒ* 厕所
Railway station *Huǒchē zhàn* 火车站
Bus station *Qìchē zhàn* 汽车站
Embassy *Dàshǐguǎn* 大使馆
Consulate *Lǐngshìguǎn* 领事馆
Passport *Hùzhào* 护照
Visa *Qiānzhèng* 签证
Pharmacy *Yàodiàn* 药店
Hospital *Yīyuàn* 医院
Doctor *Dàifu/yīshēng* 大夫/医生
Translate *Fānyì* 翻译

Left: Nanjing Road West.

Early morning/morning *Zǎoshàng/shàngwǔ*
早上/上午
Midday/afternoon/evening *Zhōngwǔ/xiàwǔ/wǎnshang*
中午/下午/晚上
Yesterday/today/tomorrow *Zuótiān/jīntiān/míngtiān*
昨天/今天/明天
Hour/day/week/month *Xiǎoshí/tiān/xīngqī/yuè*
小时/天/星期/月

Eating Out

Waiter/waitress *Fúwùyuán/ xiǎojiě* 服务员/小姐
Menu *Càidān* 菜单
Chopsticks *Kuàizi* 筷子
Knife *Dāozi* 刀子
Fork *Chāzi* 叉子
Spoon *Sháozi* 勺子
I am a vegetarian *Wǒ shì chī sù de rén* 我是吃素的人
Beer *Píjiǔ* 啤酒
Red/white wine *Hóng/bái pú táo jiǔ* 红/白葡萄酒
Green/black tea *Lǜchá/ hóngchá* 绿茶/红茶
Coffee *Kāfēi* 咖啡
Beef/pork/lamb/chicken *Niúròu/zhūròu/yángròu/jīròu* 牛肉/猪肉/羊肉/鸡肉
Spicy/sweet/sour/salty *Là/tián/suān/xián* 辣/甜/酸/咸
Can we have the bill, please *Qǐng jié zhàng/mǎidān* 请结帐/买单

Numbers

One/two/three/four/five *Yī/èr/sān/sì/wǔ*
一/二/三/四/五
Six/seven/eight/nine/ten *Liù/qī/bā/jiǔ/shí*
六/七/八/九/十
Eleven/twelve/twenty/ thirty/forty *Shíyī/shíèr/ érshí/sānshí/sìshí*
十一/十二/二十/三十/四十
Fifty/sixty/seventy/eighty/ ninety *Wǔshí/liùshí/ qīshí/bāshí/jiǔshí*
五十/六十/七十/八十/九十
One hundred *Yìbǎi* 一百
One thousand *Yìqiān* 一千

Do you have...? *Nín yǒu... ma* 您有...吗?
I want to go to... *Wǒ yào qù...* 我要去...
I want/I would like *Wǒ yào/ wǒ xiǎng yào* 我要/我想要
I want to buy... *Wǒ xiǎng mǎi...* 我想买...

Shopping

How much does it cost? *Zhège duōshǎo qián?*
这个多少钱?
Too expensive, thank you *Tài guì le, xièxie* 太贵了, 谢谢

Money, Hotels, Transport, Communications

Money *Qián* 钱
Traveller's cheque *Lǚxíng zhīpiào* 旅行支票
Credit card *Xìnyòngkǎ*
信用卡
Foreign currency *Wàihuì*
外汇券
Where can I change money? *Zài nǎr kěyǐ huàn qián?* 在哪儿可以换钱?
What is the exchange rate? *Bǐjià shì duōshǎo?*
比价是多少?
We want to stay for one *Wǒmen xiǎng zhù yì*
我们想住一(两, 三)天

(two/three) nights *(liǎng/sān) tiān*
How much is the room per day? *Fángjiān duōshǎo qián yì tiān?* 房间多少钱一天?
Room number *Fángjiān hàomǎ* 房间号码
Single room *Dānrén fángjiān* 单人房间
Double room *Shuāngrén fángjiān* 双人房间
Reception *Qiántái/fúwùtái* 前台/服务台
Key *Yàoshi* 钥匙
Luggage *Xíngli* 行李
Airport *Fēijīchǎng* 飞机场
Bus *Gōnggòng qìchē* 公共汽车
Taxi *Chūzū qìchē* 出租汽车
Bicycle *Zìxíngchē* 自行车
Telephone *Diànhuà* 电话
Telephone number *Diànhuà hàomǎ* 电话号码
Use the Internet *Shàngwǎng* 上网

Time

When? *Shénme shíhou?* 什么时候?
What time is it now? *Xiànzài jǐ diǎn zhōng?* 现在几点钟?
How long? *Duōcháng shíjiān?* 多长时间?

Museums and Galleries

Shanghai has a good selection of museums, ranging from Chinese to modern neon pop art museums, and from historical displays to glimpses into the future. From a visitor's perspective, the best feature of Shanghai's museums is location: four of the best are in People's Park. The art galleries are similarly convenient: in a single long afternoon at 50 Moganshan Road, a visitor could become deeply immersed in modern Chinese art. The city is replete with galleries featuring cutting-edge newcomers and old-guard artists.

The Bund

Shanghai Gallery of Art at Three on the Bund

3/F, Three on the Bund, 3 Zhongshan East First Road, by Guangdong Road; tel: 6321 5757; www.shanghaigalleryofart.com; 11am–9pm; free; Bus: 135, 145; map p.140 B1

The exterior of this historic building belies the slick modern interior. The gallery sits within 1,000 sq m (11,000 sq ft) of exhibition space featuring high ceilings, mixed use of marble, brick and slate, and majestic columns, all of which provide a textured base where sculptures, paintings and installation works come to life.

People's Park Area

Museum of Contemporary Art (MoCA)

Gate 7, People's Park, 231 Nanjing West Road; tel: 6327 9900; www.mocashanghai.org; daily 10am–6pm, Wed until 10pm; admission; Metro: Line 1, People's Square; Bus: 18, 71; map p.134 A2

Samuel Kung, a businessman and art patron, opened the Museum of Contemporary Art (MoCA) in September 2005 as a non-profit institution devoted to the arts. The museum was once a greenhouse, and its glass walls are intact, a setup that allows sunlight to illuminate the high-ceilinged interior space. The exhibits are mostly avant-garde, with a bias towards installation art and Chinese contemporary art.

Shanghai Art Museum

325 Nanjing Road West, in People's Park; tel: 6327 2829; www.sh-artmuseum.org.cn; daily 9am–5pm; admission; Metro: Lines 1, 2, People's Square; Bus: 23, 71; map p.134 A2

Shanghai Art Museum is housed in a stately stone structure that was once the Shanghai Race Club (see tint box, p.10). The ground floor, formerly the betting hall, now houses rotating exhibitions, while the upper floors host the permanent collection. The permanent collection includes modern Chinese oil paintings and pop art, along with a handful of more contemporary works. Chinese and other Asian artists are well represented, and overall the collection is eye-catching and modern, with signs in English and Chinese.

Shanghai Museum

201 Renmin De Dao; tel: 6372 3500; www.shanghaimuseum.

Above: Shanghai Art Museum.
Right: Shanghai Museum.

Left: Moganshan Road art district.

logical order, a thoughtful setup that allows visitors to observe artistic evolutions.

Shanghai Urban Planning and Exhibition Centre

100 Renmin Da Dao, in People's Square; tel: 6318 4477; www.supec.org; Tue–Thur 9am–5pm, Fri–Sun 9am–6pm; admission; Metro: People's Square; Bus: 46; map p.134 A2

This museum is mostly famous for its huge diorama of the streets and buildings of Shanghai in the year 2020, which is viewed from a series of suspended walkways, and for its super high-speed mini-imax film theatre, with an equally futuristic take on the city. But it also peers into the past, with some fine historical descriptions of the city, and multimedia screens that show photos taken from the same places, but decades apart, illustrating the rapid changes that have occurred in this fast-moving city.

Hongkou and Suzhou Creek

Art Scene Warehouse

2/F, Bldg 4, 50 Moganshan Road; tel: 6277 4940; www.artscene warehouse.com; Tue–Sun 10.30am–6.30pm; free; Metro: Line 1, Shanghai Railway Station, then 5-minute taxi; Bus: 13, 76, 105

Affiliated with Art Scene China and Art Scene Classic, Art Scene Warehouse features an exhibition space of 1,800 sq m (19,000 sq ft), and its minimalist features prove an effective backdrop to the fast-changing contemporary pieces on display.

BizArt

4/F, Bldg 7, 50 Moganshan Road; tel: 6277 5358; Mon–Fri 11am–

Shanghai is undergoing an artistic renaissance, as artists forge their own rules and break new ground. Generally, two broad forms have emerged: one is traditional, and has attracted a Chinese audience, and the other is pop-oriented, and has attracted an overseas following. Chinese buyers like to focus on technique and familiar forms, like landscapes and animals and other traditional subjects, sometimes with a hint of the erotic. Foreigners, however, are attracted to political pop art, often rendered in multimedia with a variety of images, and usually containing a message or statement.

net; daily 9am–5pm; free; Metro: Lines 1, 2, People's Square; Bus: 574, 71,123; map p.134 A2

With its state-of-the-art displays, detailed English signs and audio tours, this is the best of Shanghai's museums. It has a large collection of Chinese art and artefacts, displayed in 11 comfortable galleries. The building itself opened in 1995, and its collection of bronzes – mostly ancient dings, or large ceremonial vessels – is unparalleled, and it also has an eye-catching collection of the blue-and-white Ming ceramics, and of the bright, day-glo ceramics of the Qing era. Galleries are arranged in chrono-

6pm, Sat–Sun noon–6pm; free; Metro: Line 1, Shanghai Railway Station, then 5-minute taxi; Bus: 13, 76, 105

Active in the art scene for over 10 years, this gallery is known for its Compass programme, which supports young local artists. The gallery has split its exhibition space in half to provide a venue for artists in residence. And despite having the word 'biz' in the name, the gallery adheres to a not-for-profit model.

Eastlink Gallery
5/F, Bldg 6, 50 Moganshan Road; tel: 6276 9932; www.eastlink gallery.cn; Tue–Sun 10am–6pm; free; Metro: Line 1, Shanghai Railway Station, then 5-minute taxi; Bus: 13, 76, 105

Established in 1999 by Li Liang, Eastlink is considered a pioneer in Shanghai's art community, and it now operates as a commercial art gallery and a museum. The white minimalist venue measures 900 sq m (10,000 sq ft) and allows for a high degree of flexibility in the different variety of works that go on display.

ShanghART
Bldg 18, 50 Moganshan Road; tel: 6276 2818; www.shanghart. com; Tue–Sun 1–6pm; free; Metro: Line 1, Shanghai Railway Station, then 5-minute taxi; Bus: 13, 76, 105

Another stalwart of the neighbourhood, ShanghART is a leading gallery for contemporary artwork by local talent opened by Swiss national Lorenz Helbling in 1996. Today, the gallery represents over 40 of the country's most talked-about artists, who specialise in a wide range of media such as painting and sculpture, video art and performance.

Former French Concession North
James Cohan Gallery Shanghai
1/F, Bldg 1, Lane 170, Yueyang Road, between Jianguo and Yongjia Roads; tel: 5466 0825; www.jamescohan.com; Tue–Sat 10am–6pm, Sun noon–6pm, Mon by appointment; free; Metro: Line 1, Hengshan Road; map p.137 C2

Tucked inside a lane in the French Concession, this New York gallery is on the ground floor of a renovated 1930s garden villa. The parquet floor and rotunda add an elegance of the era to the contemporary exhibits, while the painted high ceilings reflect a bold and tasteful use of dramatic flair. This gallery has a reputation for showing dynamic international talent.

Leo Gallery
Ferguson Lane, 376 Wukang Road; tel: 5465 8785; www.leogallery.com.cn; Tue–Sun 11am–7pm; free; Metro: Line 1, Changshu; Bus: 926, 945; map p.136 B2

Situated in the heart of the city's diplomatic sector, this intimate gallery specialises in fine art by young international talent.

Former French Concession South
Art Labor Gallery
10–36 Yongjia Road, by Maoming Road; tel: 6431 7782; www.art laborgallery.com; Tue–Sat 11am–7pm, Sun noon–6pm; free; Metro: Line 1, Shaanxi, then 10-minute walk; Bus: 41, 104; map p.137 D2

With its picture windows offering passers-by a glimpse of the striking works inside, Art Labor Gallery is completely accessible. Founder Martin Kemble, from Canada, has aimed to showcase original works regardless of the nationality of the artist. As a result, a wide range of talent from around the world has been highlighted here. The gallery also supports artists in residence by providing a workspace located in the suburbs of Shanghai.

Beaugeste Photo Gallery
Space 519, Bldg 5, Lane 210, Taikang Road; tel: 6466 9012; www.beaugeste-gallery.com; Sat–Sun 10am–6pm, Mon–Fri by appointment only; free; Metro: Line 1, Shaanxi, then 5-minute taxi; map p.137 E2

This gallery, curated by Jean Loh, a French national and respected member of Shanghai's art community, specialises in contemporary photography and has a monthly exhibition cycle that presents the works of major photographic talent. Previous exhibits have included Marc Riboud, Thierry Girard and Wang Gang, the winner of a World Press Photo award.

Deke Erh Centre

Bldg 2, Lane 210, Taikang Road; tel: 6415 0675; www.han-yuan. com; daily 10.30am–6.30pm; free; Metro: Line 1, Shaanxi, then 5-minute taxi; map p.137 E2

Located along the main alleyway of Taikang Road, this gallery was opened by respected photographer and author Deke Erh. Famous for his excellent photos of Shanghai's colonial architecture, Erh has also published a number of books on old China and created Tibetan-themed oil paintings. A number of old Shanghai books and postcards are on sale here.

Shanghai Museum of Arts and Crafts

79 Fenyang Road, at the intersection of Fenyang and Tai Yuan roads; tel: 6431 4074; daily 9am–4pm; admission; Metro: Line 1, Changshu Road; map p.137 D3

This hidden gem is housed in a century-old neoclassical mansion in the heart of the old French Concession. Inside are some interesting displays of needlepoint and carvings and papercuts, and some craftsmen and women hard at work, but the chief attraction is the graceful old villa itself. Built in 1905, it has high ornate ceilings, stained-glass windows, spacious lawns, marble staircases and sculpted fishponds, and it is easy to imagine the lifestyles that were once enjoyed here.

Pudong

Shanghai History Museum

1 Century Boulevard; tel: 5239 2222; www.shmuseum.org/ en.php; daily 9am–3.30pm; admission; Metro: Line 2, Lujiazui; Bus: 72, 73, 251; map p.135 D4

This unassuming little museum at the base of the Oriental Pearl Tower is an unexpected treat. Through clever use of photos and recreations, and with the help of some 30,000 historical relics, it recreates the past 150 years of city history.

Especially moving are the exhibits that show existing buildings, such as the Bund and the Waibaidu Bridge, but filled with people, cars and boats from a bygone era.

Shanghai Science and Technology Museum

2000 Century Avenue; tel: 6862 2000; www.sstm.org.cn/ structure/english2/eindex; Tue–Sun 9am–5.15pm; admission; Metro: Line 2, Science and Technology Museum; Bus: 640, 794

This ultra-modern museum boasts high-tech exhibits in a new building with broad grounds, vaulting glass-and-steel ceilings and other modern touches. The displays are up-to-date, and include attractions ranging from exploding volcanoes to laser demonstrations to robots that play ping-pong, along with displays of the natural world, all with explanations in English. It has 12 huge galleries, spread over five floors, a surface area 65,000 sq m (700,000 sq ft), and two Imax 3-D theatres and an Iwerks theatre.

Music

Shanghai's music scene is evolving rapidly, particularly in the classical realm, where the city has resident orchestra and opera troupes, plus the Shanghai Conservatory of Music has earned an excellent global reputation. Shanghai also boasts sumptuous performance halls, including the Oriental Arts Centre, the Shanghai Grand Theatre and the Shanghai Concert Hall, which all have performance-filled schedules. On the nightclub front, a rock-and-roll scene is under way, but jazz is king in Shanghai, and the city has first-rate jazz clubs that attract top musicians from China and around the world.

Classical and Opera

The Shanghai Philharmonic Orchestra has carved out a reputation for solid musicianship since its establishment in 1952. It performs a regular slate of Western classical music, and it is also known for its fine renditions of Chinese orchestral works. Another troupe, the Shanghai Opera House, has a huge repertoire and performs nearly 50 concerts per year, including Chinese and Western opera, symphonies and famous Western ballets.

Music Venues

Oriental Arts Centre

425 Dingxiang Road, Pudong; tel: 6854 1234; www.shoac. com.cn; Metro: Line 2, Science and Technology Museum; Bus: 638, 640, 987

The Oriental Arts Centre opened in 2005 in Pudong as one of the finest concert halls in existence. Beautiful but also playful, the Paul Andreu-designed centre has five circular halls that resemble a five-petal flower in full bloom, or a butterfly on the wing, depending upon your perspective. The lustrous interiors, designed to evoke natural elements such as earth, forests, mountains, and sky, feature three theatres – Concert Hall, Opera Hall, and a smaller Performance Hall – all with superb sightlines and state-of-the-art acoustics that faithfully transmit the subtlest of notes and the softest of voices.

Shanghai Concert Hall

523 Yan'an Road East; tel: 6386 2836; www.shanghaiconcerthall. org/index.asp; Metro: Line 1,2, 8, People's Park; Bus: 17, 71, 126, 936; map p.134 B2

This venerable hall opened in 1930 as the Nanking Theatre, but was relocated brick by brick, beginning in 2002. It reopened in 2004 just 66m/yds away, featuring better acoustics and a roomier stage. The Oriental Arts Centre is a brighter star, but this beautiful hall remains one of the most popular concert venues in town, and showcases a rich selection of performances year-round.

Shanghai Conservatory of Music

20 Fenyang Road; tel: 6431 8542/6431 2157; Metro: Line 1, Shaanxi; Bus: 1; map p.137 D3

Students are in the spotlight at the conservatory's He Lu Ting Concert Hall throughout the semester, and performances are open to the public free of charge – pick up your tickets in room 718. Concert schedules vary depending on the courses being offered, and on occasion, visiting musicians from Europe, North America and Asia present perform-

Left and below: JZ Club.

corner of Fuxing Road; tel: 6437 7110; Tue–Sun 7.30pm–late, live music from 9.30pm on weekdays, and from 10.30pm on weekends; Metro: Line 1, Changshu; Bus: 96, 506; map p.136 C3
The longest-running jazz club in town, Cotton Club is a local institution that presents skilled bands and tight musicianship to enthusiastic crowds. Low ceilings, lots of smoke and an aura of inky darkness add to the atmosphere, although the house band does sometimes blur the line between jazz and blues.

JZ Club
46 Fuxing Road West; tel: 6431 0269; www.jzclub.cn; daily 8pm–late; Metro: Line 1, Changshu; Bus: 96, 113; map p.136 B3
While most 'jazz' venues in Shanghai play pop music and blues and even show tunes, JZ remains true to its roots, with an ongoing selection of superlative jazz musicians from China and overseas, plus a fine house band. The club has a friendly two-storey layout, where listeners are almost literally on top of the stage. Book early for top bands.
For other live-music venues See Nightlife, p.92

Live music clubs in Shanghai tend to have the lifespan of a firefly: they emerge, grow wings and glow for a few months, and then expire. The jazz clubs listed here have withstood the test of time; to find the others, check one of the local listings magazines.

---

ances together with their students.

Shanghai Grand Theatre
300 People's Avenue; tel: 6372 8702; Metro: Line 1, 2, 8, People's Square; Bus: 17, 18, 20, 109; map p.134 A2
The Grand Theatre opened in 1998 in People's Park, and while it is drab on the outside, it is remarkable on the inside. Designed by the company ARTE Charpentier, it has one of the biggest and best equipped stages in existence, and it plays host to extravagant musicals such as The Lion King, and Cats, while smaller performances are held in cosier side theatres.

Jazz
Cotton Club
1416 Huaihai Road Central,

Nightlife

Midnight is the witching hour in Shanghai, when the city's night owls start to prowl the streets. The clubs of choice change frequently, as newer, bigger and better-designed challengers throw open their doors to compete with the reigning champions. The result is a dynamic club culture that is packed with after-dark temptations, ranging from lounge bars where patrons lie prone like Roman emperors, to DJ-fuelled dance clubs that sparkle and surge with energy, to compact and crowded live music bars where the bands play long into the night. Shanghai is a party that doesn't stop until the sun peers over the Huangpu River, and sometimes not even then.

Nightclubs

Bar Rouge

7/F, 18 Zhongshan Road East No.1; tel: 6339 1199; www.bar-rouge-shanghai.com; Sun–Thur 6pm–2am, Fri–Sat 6pm–4.30am; Metro: Line 2, Nanjing East; map p.140 B3

Formerly on the cutting edge, and now a well-worn venue, this big Bund 18 hotspot continues to draw upscale crowds with its cranberry-coloured lounges, hot red lighting and professional DJs, and despite its famously snooty service. The best tables are on a patio overlooking the Huangpu River; be sure to reserve if you wish to sit outside.

Dragon Club

156 Fenyang Road, near Taojiang Lu; tel: 6433 2187; www.dragonclub.com.cn; Wed–Thur 10pm–4am, Fri–Sat 10pm–8am; Metro: Line 1, Changshu; Bus: 49, 96; map p.137 C2

Five staff DJs and a string of top-notch international guest spinners keep the party going at this very late-night club, which doesn't really rev up until after 2am, when other bars start to close. Expect house music downstairs and hip-hop on the second floor, and expect some drunken behaviour too, since this is the last place open every night.

El Mojito

501 Dagu Road, by Shimen Road; tel: 5375 0800; daily 5pm–1am; Bus: 36, 41; map p.133 E1

El Mojito is dedicated entirely to the art of salsa dancing, complete with hot Latino music, a spicy atmosphere and wet, refreshing drinks. It is not a place for wallflowers, but if you can't dance salsa, there is good news: El Mojito also offers lessons.

Lan Club

102 Guangdong Road; tel: 6323 8029; www.lan-global.com; 11am–late; Bus: tunnel line 9; map p.140 B1

This beautifully designed newcomer is a vertical four-floor party palace with dance space, lounge, restaurant, rooftop garden, private rooms, astronomically high ceilings and friendly service. Dressed up in vibrant reds and blacks, and featuring stylish birdcages, coloured lanterns, mosaic mirrors and other chic Chinoiserie, it established itself as a firm Bund favourite soon after its 2008 opening.

M1NT

318 Fuzhou Road; tel: 6391 2811; www.M1NT.com.cn; Mon–Sat 6pm–late; Metro: Line 2, Nanjing East; map p.134 B3

Shark tanks, Bund views, beautiful people and more in this lavish club perched atop a 24-storey building five blocks from the Huangpu River. Entertainments include seasoned DJs, a spacious dance floor, bar, restaurant, rooftop party area and superb modern design. M1NT claims to be members-only, but it isn't; go before 9.30pm and you will be ushered right in.

M2

5/F, Plaza 66, 1266 Nanjing Road West; tel: 6288 6222; www.museshanghai.cn; Sun–Thur 8pm–3am, Fri–Sat 8pm–5am; Metro: Line 2, Nanjing West; map p.134 A3

Left: Shanghai's nightlife has an international flavour. but hotel bars (**below**) still play a big role.

No. 88

2/F, 291 Fumin Road, in Wujing Mansion; tel: 6136 0288; www. no88bar.com; daily 8.30pm–6am; Metro: Line 1, Changshu; map p.137 C4

A nice mid-market antidote to the ultra-upscale clubs elsewhere in the city, the expansive 88 club is a non-stop visual and aural feast that is over the top but plenty of fun. The decor is metallic, and everywhere are propellers, brass fittings, pipes and other Captain Nemo-style decorations, along with leather sofas, velvet drapes and plaid-clad waitresses, and further in, a DJ station and a live music stage.

The Shelter

5 Yongfu Road, near Fuxing Road West; tel: 6347 0400; Wed–Sun 9pm–late; Metro: Line 1, Changshu; Bus: 96, 113; map p.136 A3

Every city needs a nightclub like The Shelter: concrete walls, black paint, rock-bottom cocktail prices (Rmb20 for a mixed drink) and consistently good music, much of it alternative and hip-hop. This former bomb shelter draws a youthful alternative crowd, who are joined

Shanghai's brightest collection of nightlife is on **Tongren Road**, between Yan'an and Nanjing West roads. This lively slice of party heaven features more than 20 nightclubs, enjoy it while you can. This area is rumored to be closing in time for Expo 2010. Another cluster of drinking venues is in Xintiandi, while in the former French Concession, the clubs are more or less evenly scattered throughout the neighbourhood, with a small but busy clutch of beer bars on the corner of Hengshan and Gao'an roads.

Muse at Park 97

2 Gaolan Road, Lan Kwai Fong at Park 97 in Fuxing Park; tel: 5383 2328; www.museshanghai.cn; Sun–Thur 8pm–2am, Fri–Sat 8pm–late; Metro: Line 1, Huangpi; map p.137 E4

The brightest star in the small galaxy of clubs that sits just inside Fuxing Park, the recently renovated Muse is a heaving, throbbing dance club with brash decor and an equally brash clientele of well-heeled Hong Kongers, nouveau riche mainlanders, expats, wannabees and other beautiful people. International DJs and the occasional Asian celebrity add to the see-and-be-seen atmosphere.

Even by Shanghai standards, M2 is a monument to conspicuous consumption, where well-heeled Shanghai and Hong Kong clientele, plus the occasional model or local celeb, dance in light-spangled splendour beneath a mirrored disco ball, or lounge on acres of cranberry-red cushions, or hang out at the long, curved ivory-white bar. Including restaurant, lounge, club, and outdoor balcony, M2 can hold 2,000 guests.

by locals looking for a good time in unpretentious surroundings.

Sin Lounge

23/F, Want Want Plaza, 211 Shimen 1 Road, next to Four Seasons Hotel; tel: 6267 7779; www.sinshanghai.com; 6pm–late; Metro: Line 2, Nanjing West; map p.133 D2

If you visit only one club in Shanghai, make it Sin, because this newcomer perfectly encapsulates Shanghai nightlife in one remarkable package. A juicy red apple at the door, a snake-like entry hall, Garden of Eden jungle decor, massive floor space and high-flying city views await visitors, along with classy cocktails and deep, soulful house and tech-house music.

Cocktail Lounges

Bar Constellation

86 Xinle Road, near Xiangyang Road North; tel: 5404 0970; 7pm–2am; Metro: Line 1, Shaanxi; map p.137 D4

This narrow cocktail bar – booths on one side, bar on the other – is much loved for its fine mixology. Its classic cocktails are perfectly balanced and never too sweet, and whisky and other drinks on the rocks are served 'Japanese style' with a single large ice cube, so they stay cold without getting watery.

Bed

4/F, 456 Nanjing Road West; tel: 6359 5367; www.bed-shanghai.com; Mon–Fri 11.30am–2am, Sat–Sun 5pm–2am; Metro: Line 2, Nanjing West; map p.133 D2

The name says it all: sink into the deeply cushioned red booths that ring the beautifully backlit bar, and unwind in a soul-soothing embrace of well-crafted cocktails, modern surrounds and lounge tempo music. An outdoor balcony offers equally relaxing views of Nanjing Road, including the classic clock tower of Shanghai Art Museum.

Lounge 18

4/F, 18 Zhongshan East Road No. 1, near Nanjing Road East; tel: 6323 8399; www.lounge18.com; Mon–Fri noon–2am; Sat–Sun noon–4am; Metro: Line 2, Nanjing East; map p.140 B3

This sophisticated Bund 18 venue is a kinder and gentler alternative to the seething and competitive Bar Rouge just upstairs, and its fine lounge DJs, classy mixed crowd, elegant dress code and ample space are more suited to relaxing than to dancing.

Velvet Lounge

913 Julu Road, near Changshu Road; tel: 5403 2976; www.cosmogroup.cn; Sun–Thur 6pm–3am, Fri–Sat 6pm–5am; Bus: 15, 49; map p.136 C4

With its effortless combination of comfort and class, this is the number one lounge bar among in-the-know locals. Good cocktails, great pizzas, atmospheric nooks and crannies, and friendly if overworked waiting staff generate a warm and welcoming vibe. Come very early or very late if you want a seat at weekends.

Gay and Lesbian

D2

505 Zhongshan Road South, near the Bund; tel: 6152 6543; www.clubd2.cn; Wed–Sat

Scams perpetrated on unwary nightclubbers, especially late at night, are a fact of life in Shanghai. The most common tricks are padding the bill with extra drinks, or adding it up wrong – always in their favour. Another scam, less common but harder to deal with, is the 'fake Rmb100 bill trick.' After you pay, a waitress and two or three burly bouncers will follow you out of the bar with a fake Rmb100 note, and demand a real one in exchange. Your choice – submit to the scam, or go to a police station, and wait many hours for a resolution.

8.30pm–late; Bus: 65, 305; map p.135 D1
Expect techno-dance music, smoke, laser beams and a giant dance floor filled with heaving bodies in this new Cool Docks hotspot located in a once-derelict strip of Huangpu River waterfront.

Left: Sin Lounge. **Above:** a night out in Huaihai Road.

Top techno DJs often arrive from Asia and elsewhere, and D2 also presents a steady stream of lively theme parties for those who like to dress up.

Eddy's Bar
1877 Huaihai Road Central; tel: 6282 0521; Mon–Thur 8pm–2am, Fri–Sun 8pm–3am; Metro: Line 1, Changshu; map p.137 D4
Small, popular and well established, Eddy's is a neighbourhood bar with cosy red and golden lighting, an early-arriving and quite cosmopolitan crowd, and concrete walls covered in Asian-themed art and collectibles. Known for its good music and expertly rendered cocktails.

Frangipani
399 Dagu Road, near Shimen Road; tel: 5375 0084; www.frangipanibar.com; 6pm–2am; Bus: 36, 41; map p.133 E1
Secluded candlelit tables, dim light and post-industrial decor greet visitors in this rel-
ative newcomer on Dagu Road, a new entertainment zone not far from People's Park. Drinks at Frangipani are reasonable, the appetisers are tasty, and the couches are comfortable.

Shanghai Studio
Building 4, 1950 Huaihai Road Central, near Wukang Road; tel: 6283 1043; www.shanghai-studio.com; 9pm–late; Metro: Line 1, Hengshan; Bus: 26; map p.136 B2
A labyrinthine concrete lair in a former bomb shelter, Shanghai Studio is known for its friendly staff, stiff drinks, warm and welcoming vibe, and over-the-top costume parties. Expect a maze of modestly sized rooms, many of them featuring offbeat Asian art, a small dance floor, and a mixed local and expat crowd.

Revues
Cabaret
3/F, 6 Zhongshan East Road No. 1, near Guangdong Road; tel: 6329 7333; 9pm–3am; Metro:

91

Line 1, Nanjing East; map p.140 B2

A unique and sophisticated stage show that offers a smooth blend of jazz and cabaret – think Moulin Rouge – in a classy tribute to the 1930s. The gentle nostalgia is presented in a subtle but upscale setting, as you would expect given its Bund 6 address.

Chinatown

471 Zhapu Road, near Wujin Road, Hongkou District; tel: 6258 2078; www.chinatown shanghai.com; Wed–Sat 8pm–2am; Bus: 14

Formerly a Japanese Shinto shrine built in 1931, China-town is now a three-story club filled with dark wood, velvet drapes, gilded bal-conies, and rich ruby over-tones that recreate the storied past of Shanghai. The revue, launched by New York choreographers Gos-ney and Kallman, features a parade of gorgeous cos-tumes, light-hearted skits, silly jokes, and song-and-dance numbers that com-bine cabaret, burlesque, comedy and vaudeville into a single seamless show.

Live Music

Brown Sugar Jazz Club

Building 15, Lane 181, Taicang Road, North Block, Xintiandi; tel: 5382 8998; www.brownsugar live.com/shanghai/main.html; Mon–Fri 6pm–3am, Sat–Sun 6pm–4am; Metro: Line 1, Huangpi; map p.134 A1

Big, bold and beautiful, Brown Sugar is a belt-'em-out music hall with super-high ceilings, brick walls, a roomy stage in front and deep, extensive interiors in the rear, anchored by a circu-lar bar. The music here is not jazz, but Americana: blues, jazz, pop, showtunes, R&B, and more, laid down by a slick house band and often spiced up by visiting singers.

Most Chinese restaurants stop serving dinner by 9pm, but there are exceptions: Charmant, Hengshan Café, Sichuan Citizen, Tsui Wah and XinJiang Style Restaurant all serve until 2am or later. But Shanghai's favourite late-night grazing venue is the well-located **City Diner** (142 Tongren Road; tel: 6289 3699; www.citydiner.cn). Just a block from the Tongren Road nightlife strip, City Diner serves burgers, fries, bacon and eggs, and other American-style comfort food 24 hours a day.

House of Blues and Jazz

60 Fuzhou Lu, near Fujian Mid-dle Road; tel: 6323 2779; daily 4.30pm–3am; Metro: Line 2, Nanjing East; Bus: 49, 123; map p.134 B3

This gem of club opened in 2008 in a renovated mansion on a quiet Bund backstreet, and quickly attracted a firm following with its unpreten-

tious but upscale atmosphere and excellent bands that play soul-infused blues and jazz. Design-wise, its long wood-grained bar, hardwood walls and floors, and Art Deco-style fittings pay tribute to Shanghai's earlier jazz era.

Live Bar
721 Kunming Road, near Tong-bei Lu; tel: 2833 6764; www.chinalivebar.com; 8pm–2am; Metro: Line 4, Dalian

One of Shanghai's most pro-gressive live music clubs and a staple of the Shanghai music scene, Live Bar offers a lively mix of rock and roll, metal, punk and other guitar-heavy genres. At weekends, it showcases up-and-coming Chinese bands, and while it is in the rather distant Yangpu district north of Hongkou, it makes up for the cab ride with low cover charges and inexpensive drinks.

LOgO
13 Xingfu Road, near Fahuazhen Road; tel: 6281 5646; www.logoshanghai.net; 8.30pm–late; Bus: 76

A youthful favourite that is much-loved for its consistent presentation of alternative music, including electronic, punk rock and metal, and for its gritty, smoky, laid-back interiors, low drinks prices and rea-sonable cover charges. The house is packed on weekends, so expect big crowds of 20- and 30-somethings gathered for a good time.

Left and above: Shanghai by night.

93

Pampering

Massage parlours, nail and beauty salons and spas have proliferated in Shanghai in the last five years, ranging from no-frills bare-bones operations to plush and decadent five-star treatments. For example, you can get a haircut for Rmb5, or spend thousands in a stylish salon. Luxury hotels dominate the top end of the market, with world-class spa facilities and well-trained practitioners, but a large middle market is developing with the spread of home-grown chain outlets. Added to this mix are traditional Chinese treatments, such as acupuncture, qigong and cupping, which can be therapeutic as well as relaxing.

Beauty Treatments

Anantara, Puli Hotel & Spa
Level 3, 1 Changde Road, near Yanan Road; tel: 2216 6899; www.thepuli.com; daily 10am–10pm; Metro: Line 2, Jing'an Temple; map p.132 C1
The Thai-based Anantara Spa Group is behind this beautiful spa at the Puli. Its speciality treatments are inspired by the properties of tea and include green tea purification, white tea moisturiser, rose tea beautification, and chrysanthemum tea cleansing packages ranging from 160 to 190 minutes for Rmb1,520 and up.

Apsara Spa
457 Shaanxi North Road, near Beijing West Road; tel: 6258

5580; 11am–midnight; Metro: Line 2, Nanjing West; map p.13 C2
Pudong location: 290 Jinyan Road, near Jingxiu Road; tel: 5059 0301; daily 10am–10pm; Metro: Line 2, Shanghai Science and Technology Museum
This Cambodian-style spa has a distinct Indochina feel with its white silk cushions and dark wooden floors. Its wellness-inspired body treatments include chocolate therapy and red wine baths, but its most popular treatments are the oil and aromatherapy massages. Speciality services include waxing and henna tattooing.

Chi Spa, Shangri-La Hotel
6/F, Tower 2, 33 Fucheng Road, Pudong; tel: 5877 1503; daily 10am–midnight; Metro: Line 2, Lujiazui; map p.135 D3
One of the city's finest spas, Chi takes a holistic approach to body treatments, requiring visitors to fill out a thorough questionnaire on personal preferences. The soft lighting and quiet long hallways invite visitors to leave the busy, noisy city below. Private suites feature a shower, bathroom, changing area, bathtub and one or two massage tables. The signature treatment is its Aroma Vitality massage that combines Japanese shiatsu, Swedish massage and a detoxifying facial (two hours and 40 minutes for up to Rmb2,000).

Dashing Diva
423 Julu Road, near Shanxi Road; tel: 5228 1078; www. dashingdiva.com.cn; daily 10am–10pm; Metro: Line 1, Shaanxi; Bus: 24; map p.133 D1
This tiny location is part of an international franchise chain and is a combination nail salon and boutique decked out in hot pink. Its underlying philosophy is that nails are a form of creative self-expression. Dashing Diva's own branded products are used, and practitioners adhere to international hygiene standards.

Diva Life Nail & Beauty Lounge
266 Ruijin Road, between Jianguo and Taikang Roads;

> **Foot massage**, or reflexology, involves the stimulation of pressure points in the feet that correspond to different organs of the body. The pain involved in such massages is meant to be therapeutic, but masseuses will lighten up the pressure if asked to do so.

Left and below: Shui Urban Spa *(see p.96)*.

One of the best-known chains in Shanghai, Dragonfly has 10 locations across the city. It offers full spa treatments in private rooms including facials, a variety of different types of massages, body treatments, and nail services for both men and women. Gentle new-age music, a quiet atmosphere, serene staff and Thai-flavoured decor typify these outlets. One of its more popular treatments is Happy Landing, a massage for the jetlagged.

tel: 5465 7291; daily 10am–10pm; Metro: Line 1, Shaanxi Road, then taxi; Bus: 24, 26, 146; map p.137 E2

Fuxing Park location: 66 Nanchang Road, near Yandang Road; tel: 6384 2033; www.mydiva life.com; daily 10am–10pm; Metro: Line 1, between Shaanxi and Huangpu; map p.137 E4

Pudong location: 1/F, Tower 3 German Centre, 88 Keyuan Road, near Longdong Avenue, Pudong; tel: 2898 6078; daily 10am–10pm; Metro: Line 2, Zhangjiang High Tech Park

This salon has three venues, one in a renovated lane-house near Taikang Road, another on Nanchang Road near Fuxing Park, and a larger outlet in Pudong that also offers hair-styling and hair-colouring services. Chinese-, Japanese- and English-speaking staff provide an extensive selection spa, and therapeutic and beauty treatments for men and women include waxing, scrubs and wraps. Popular treatments include the Head-to-Toe Spa (Rmb498 for a 45-minute body mas-

sage and 30-minute foot massage) and the Executive Manicure for men (Rmb300 for 70 minutes).

Dragonfly

20 Donghu Road, between Huaihai and Xinle Roads; tel: 5405 0008; www.dragonfly.net.cn; daily 10am–2am; Metro: Line 1, Changshu; map p.137 D4

206 Xinle Road; tel: 5403 9982; daily 10am–2am, nail service until 11pm; Metro: Line 1, Changshu; map p.137 C4

84 Nanchang Road, near Yandang Road; tel: 5386 0060; daily 10am–midnight; Metro: Line 1 between Shaanxi and Huangpi; map p.137 E4

Frangipani

174 Xiangyang South Road, near Fuxing Middle Road; tel: 6474 5345; www.frangipani-shanghai.com; daily 10am–10pm; Metro: Line 1, Shaanxi; map p.137 D3

204 Xinle Road; tel: 5403 0227; Metro: Line 1, Shaanxi; map p.137 C4

Hongqiao location: 3305 Hongmei Road, near Huaguang; tel: 5422 2984; 9am–10am; Metro: Line 2, Loushanguan, then 10-minute taxi

This chain of nail spas has four locations that are easily

Chinese massage differs from Swedish massage in that it does not use oil. Masseuses typically place a thin cotton sheet over the customer and perform full-body, deep-tissue massage starting from the head or neck and working down the length of the back, then front. Treatment may also include some manipulation and pulling of limbs to loosen the joints, and then it is finished off with rapid clapping on the back and shoulders with cupped hands, which makes a loud, satisfying noise and is said to promote circulation.

Acupuncture is used to treat a wide range of complaints, from weight loss to headaches to back pain. Needles are inserted in specific points just below the skin that correlate to points of the body, stimulating circulation and easing muscle strain. Some practitioners will increase the effectiveness of the treatment by clamping on electrodes to deliver small electrical currents, which is not as painful as it looks or sounds.

recognised by the distinctive white decor dotted with splashes of bright colour. Standard manicures and pedicures for men and women are on offer, as well as more specialised treatments such as gel and acrylic nails, foot massage, and ginger soy treatment for hands and feet. Prices range from Rmb105 for a basic manicure to Rmb500 for gel nails.

Shui Urban Spa

5/F, Ferguson Lane, 374 Wukang Road, near Taian Road; tel: 6126 7800; www.shuiurbanspa. com.cn; daily 11am–9am, Sun until 7pm, closed Mon; Metro: Line 1, Changshu, then 5-minute taxi; map p.136 B2

This white-on-white spa features a welcoming atmosphere and English-speaking staff. Shui is one of the few locations in Shanghai that offers pre- and post-natal massages, and can customise treatments for group packages.

Blind Massage

Many places employ blind masseurs who have been specially trained to provide basic Chinese-style massages and foot massages. These venues are usually on the lower end of the cost scale, but offer decent services in basic conditions.

Fei Ning Massage Centre of the Blind

597-A8 Fuxing Middle Road, near Maoming Road; tel: 6437 8378; daily noon–12.30am; Metro: Line 1, Shaanxi; map p.137 D3

This no-frills massage parlour offers Chinese-style massages and foot massages in a dimly lit communal room for Rmb45 per hour and Rmb90 for two hours. The receptionist can speak basic English.

Shuang Caihong

45 Yongjia Road, near Shaanxi Road; tel: 6473 4000; daily noon–midnight; Metro: Line 1, Shaanxi; Bus: 41, 104; map p.137 D3

Jinan location: 426 Yuyuan Road; tel: 6211 7146; daily noon–midnight; Metro: Line 2, Jinan; Bus: 20, 48, 138; map p.132 B1

Rates are Rmb40 for a 45-minute massage, Rmb60 for a 68-minute massage. Foot massages are Rmb55 for a full hour, which can be combined with a 45-minute body massage for a total of Rmb95.

Traditional Chinese Treatments

Body and Soul Medical Clinic

14/F, Anji Plaza, 760 Xizang South Road, near Jiangguo Road; tel: 5101 9262; www.bodyandsoul.com.cn; Mon, Wed, Fri 9am–6pm, Tue, Thur 9am–8pm, Sat–Sun 10am–3pm; Metro: Line 8, Lujiabang; map p.137 D2

This unique clinic employs trained professionals who take both Western and Chinese approaches to treat injuries and ailments. Estab-

Left and above left: tea and a symbol of good luck. **Above:** its more modern interpretation at Shile Fei Fei.

Tui-na is the oldest form of Chinese massage therapy, and it adheres to the concept of eight meridians where *qi* (energy) passes through. Blocked *qi* causes pain and health problems, and to solve them, the treatment requires use of traction, massage, and rolling or pressing to stimulate acupressure points and meridians.

lished by German-born Dr Doris Rathgeber, the clinic provides a thorough consultation and treatments that include acupuncture, *tui-na* massage and physiotherapy. Initial consultation fee is Rmb850, with acupuncture treatments starting at Rmb570. Languages spoken include English, Chinese, German and Spanish.

Qigong Institute of Shanghai – VIP Clinic

3/F, 218 Nanchang Road, near Ruijin Road; tel: 5306 4832; Mon–Sat 8am–4.30pm; Metro: Line 1, Shaanxi; map p.137 E4

Located in a renovated lanehouse, this clinic has VIP services on the top floor catering to English-speakers

and those who are willing to pay a premium to avoid a long queue (about Rmb200 depending on the treatment required). Services include qigong, acupuncture (with disposable needles) and cupping.

Shile Fei Fei Xiang Spa

Bldg 1, 599 Fangdian Road, near Jinxiu Road, Pudong; tel: 5033 9113; www.jjtshile.com; daily noon–10pm; Metro: Line 2, Century Park, then 5-minute taxi; Bus: 602, 640

Shile, which means 10 pleasures in Chinese, is a lifestyle centre featuring first-rate spa facilities combined with traditional Chinese treatments. Tastefully decorated with a minimalist hand, the spa has three double rooms where two people can enjoy their treatments at the same time, as well as four single rooms. Fei Fei Xiang Classic is their signature treatment and is designed to stimulate all five senses. It includes a bath or shower, foot massage, body massage, an hour facial and tea with sesame pudding for Rmb1,075.

97

Parks and Gardens

With space at such a premium, Shanghai has fewer parks than many other major cities, but its park culture is well entrenched. Used as an extension of their courtyards, parks serve as a place where people go to socialise, read, play chess and perform t'ai chi at dawn, and ballroom dancing at dusk. Some, such as Fuxing Park, are places where Chinese people practise their English, or, for foreigners, their Chinese. While many of the larger parks charge entry fees, the smaller inner-city parks are free of charge, and are generally more crowded.

Century Park

Gate 1, 1001 Jinxiu Road, Pudong; tel: 5833 5621; daily 7am–5pm; admission; Metro: Line 2, Century Park

Shanghai's largest park, Century Park is divided into seven sections interlinked with pathways. It has a miniature golf course, a lake where you can rent boats, and it is one of the only parks in the city where you can rent and ride a bike.

Changfeng Park

Gate 4, 21 Changfeng Park, 451 Daduhe Road; tel: 5281 8888/ 6286 6399; daily 6am–5.30pm; admission; www.oceanworld. com.cn (Chinese only)

Changfeng Park is one of the city's older parks and houses

In addition to t'ai chi and ballroom dancing, a common sight in many parks is people showing off their **calligraphy** with water instead of paint on walkways. Those with particular talent usually draw a crowd, who watch and admire, until the characters fade and evaporate.

Ocean World, an aquatic entertainment centre.

Fuxing Park

105 Yandang Road; south entry on Fuxing and Chongqing Roads, west entry on Gaolan Road near Sinan Road; daily 6am–6pm; map p.137 E4

This popular park is located smack in the middle of the French Concession, and it includes a French garden, fountains, plenty of amusement park rides, and a large pond. The former residence of Sun Yat-sen is located near the west entrance.

Gongqing Forest Park

2000 Jungong Road; tel: 6574 0586/6532 8194; www.shgqsl. com; admission; daily 6am–5pm; Bus: 102 to South Gate; 124, 841 or 147 to West Gate; Metro: Line 8, Shiguang Road

This giant park is big enough to make you forget you are in a busy metropolis. You can rent a barbecue pit or enjoy amusement park rides, and it has a dozen small cabins that are available for overnight rental. Other features include horseback riding, pedal boat rentals, and walking paths galore.

Clockwise from left: People's Park; Yuyuan Garden; Century Park.

cinating Chinese medicinal garden and a quaint and curious bonsai display.

Yuyuan Garden
218 An Ren Street; daily 8.30am–5pm; admission; map p.135 C2

Yuyuan is a delightful Ming-era garden filled with ponds, pagodas, graceful arched bridges, winding footpaths and other Chinese garden delights. If possible, hire a guide who can explain the precise geometry and landscaping of the park. Entrance is past the bridge of nine turns.

Zhongshan Park
780 Changning Road; daily 6am–5pm

This park is cherished for its large grass area where visitors can picnic, play badminton, throw frisbees and fly kites. It also features Fundazzle, an indoor play area for kids with a giant ball pit, and a handful of amusement park rides.

People's Park
231 Nanjing East Road; tel: 6372 0626; daily 6am–6pm; Metro: Lines 1, 2, 8, People's Park; map p.134 A3

Built as a horse-racing track in 1863 and converted into a park in 1951, People's Park is home to four of Shanghai's top museums. The northern section, with its lotus ponds, rock gardens and lake, is by far the most calm and peaceful.

SEE ALSO MUSUEMS AND GALLERIES, P.82–3

Shanghai Botanical Garden
1111 Longwu Road; daily 9am–4pm; admission

The Shanghai Botanical Garden covers about 80 hectares (200 acres) and includes special exhibits of orchids, peonies, roses, bamboo and osmanthus, along with a fas-

Restaurants

Few cities on earth can match Shanghai for its range and variety of food. Excellent sit-down meals of meat dumplings or soup noodles, with a pot of hot tea, can be had for handful of loose change. Meanwhile, at the high end, the world's top chefs have flocked to Shanghai, where they have opened elegant flagship venues that serve some of the most refined, delicious and expensive cuisine on the planet. And in the affordable middle lies a rich treasure trove of regional Chinese cuisines and Western selections from around the globe, and many of them are served in surprising venues that could only be found in Shanghai.

The Bund

Jean Georges

4/F, 3 Zhong Shang East No. 1 Road, Three on the Bund; tel: 6321 7733; www.threeonthe bund.com; Mon–Sat 11.30am–2.30pm, Sun until 3pm, 6–11pm; $$$$; Metro: Line 2, Nanjing East; map p.140 B1

This classy Bund institution is the epitome of refined elegance, a world of just-right ingredients expertly mixed and matched, and guaranteed to set the taste buds tingling with creative flavour combinations. Seasoned foodies swear that this is the best of celebrity chef Jean-Georges Vongerichten's many venues.

Laris

6/F, 3 Zhong Shang East No. 1 Road, Three on the Bund; tel: 6321 9922; www.threeonthe bund.com; daily 11.30am–2.30pm, 6–10.30pm; $$$; Metro: Line 2, Nanjing East; map p.140 B1

The slick white marble interior is the setting for an avant-garde menu, with well-executed foams and fusion fare and a very good raw bar, brought to you by locally famous chef David Laris, who is also a renowned chocolatier.

Lost Heaven on the Bund

17 Yan An East Road; tel: 6330 0967; www.lostheaven.com.cn; daily 11.30am–2.30pm, 6–10.30pm; $$; Metro: Line 2, Nanjing East, then taxi; map p.140 B1

You may get lost in the vast, lush interiors of this 'Mountain Mekong' restaurant, which serves recipes and ingredients from northern Thailand, Burma and Yunnan province in a luxurious, three-storey setting near the Bund waterfront. Don't miss the Yunnan jungle-themed bar on the top floor.

M on the Bund

7/F, 5 Zhong Shan East No. 1 Road; tel: 6350 9988; www.m-restaurantgroup.com; daily 11.30am–2.30pm, 6–10.30pm; $$$; Metro: Line 2, Nanjing East; map p.140 B2

This time-honoured venue has become famous for its honest Australian-inspired cuisine, featuring fresh ingredients and straightforward preparations, served in a classy Bund building. Book an outdoor table during good weather, and be sure to try the slow-baked salt-encrusted lamb.

Mr and Mrs Bund

6/F, Bund 18, Zhongshan East One Road; tel: 6323 9898; www.mmbund.com; daily 6.30–10.30pm, open later for drinks; $$$; Metro: Line 1, Nanjing East; map p.140 B3

Shanghai celebrity chef Paul Pairet prepares modern French food in this Bund 18 hotspot, but with a twist; he was known for creating the ultimate fusion menu in his previous position at Jade on 36, and each of these dishes delivers a tiny touch of the unexpected.

Price for a two-course dinner per person, with one drink:
$ less than $15
$$ $15–30
$$$ $30–60
$$$$ more than $60

Left: Jean Georges. **Below:** Lost Heaven on the Bund.

Old Town

Lubolang

115 Yuyuan Road near Mid-Lake Teahouse, Yuyuan Garden; tel: 6328 0602/6355 7509; daily 7am–10pm; $$; Metro: Line 8, Laoshimen, then taxi; map p.133 C2

This rambling, old-school Shanghainese restaurant has prime views of the Mid-Lake Teahouse, curt but efficient old waiters, and a menu filled with Shanghainese favourites, including lion's-head meatballs, red-cooked pork and steamed pomfret.

Visitors in search of a culinary adventure may want to weigh their options along **Yunnan Road South** between Yan'an Road East and Jinlin Road East. A wide variety of Chinese restaurants are here, and they range from regular noodle-and-dumpling spots to seafood restaurants complete with aquarium tanks full of sea creatures, and from Xinjiang hotpot joints with their burning charcoal urns to fat and crispy Beijing duck. English menus and English-speaking staff are rare in this neighbourhood, but most of these restaurants will welcome hungry tourists.

New Heights

7/F, Three on the Bund, 3 Zhongshan East No.1 Road; tel: 6321 0909; www.threeonthebund.com; daily 11am–2.30pm, 5.30–10.30pm, bar: 11.30–1am; $$; Metro: Line 2, Nanjing East; map p.140 B1

In 2009 New Heights renovated and moved upscale, so it is not the bargain it once was, but it still occupies a niche as one of the most affordable restaurants on the Bund waterfront. The food is contemporary Asian, and the views from the wraparound balcony are unbeatable.

Sun with Aqua

2/F, 6 Zhongshan East No. 1 Road; tel: 6339 2779; $$; daily 11.30am–2.30pm, 6–10pm, bar open late; Metro: Line 1, Nanjing East; map p.140 B2

The Bund's first Japanese restaurant is a dazzling spot, where a shark aquarium entertains diners, as does an open kitchen where the chefs perform a contemporary take on Japanese cuisine, including excellent barbecued beef iand crispy salt-grilled cod.

Nan Xiang

85 Yuyuan Road near Mid-Lake Teahouse, Yuyuan Garden; tel: 6355 4206; daily 7am–8pm; $; Metro: Line 8, Laoshimen, then taxi; map p.135 C2

This packed and busy three-storey venue is ultra-popular with Chinese tourists, and it has long queues and a reputation for serving the best steamed buns in town. It is stratified by floor, with takeout on the first floor, a sit-down diner on the second serving basic *baozi*, and on the third floor it serves dumplings with crab roe and other elaborate fillings.

People's Park Area

Café du Metro

19 Nanjing West Road, at Exit 10 of People's Square Station; tel: 6327 3091; Mon–Fri 9am–10pm, Sat–Sun 11am–10pm; $; Metro: Lines 1, 2, People's Square; map p.134 A3

This little-known but much-loved bistro is in the maze of Metro tunnels beneath People's Park, where a French chef turns out excellent French diner food – pâté, chicken, beefsteak, frites, bread and cheese – at excellent prices. It is an institution in the French community.

Kathleen's 5 Rooftop Restaurant and Bar

325 Nanjing Xi Lu, top floor of Shanghai Art Museum; tel: 6327 2221/6327 0591; www.kathleens5.com.cn; daily 11.30am–10.30pm; $$; Metro:

Price for a two-course dinner per person, with one drink:
$ less than $15
$$ $15–30
$$$ $30–60
$$$$ more than $60

Lines 1, 2, People's Square; map p.134 A2

This rooftop restaurant serving Continental cuisine at the Shanghai Art Museum has stunning views of People's Park. At lunch it attracts a business crowd, and in the evening couples sip wine and soak up the ambiance. Kathleen's should not be missed, especially to enjoy the sunset with drink in hand.

Xintiandi

Crystal Jade

2/F, South Block, Lane 123, Xinye Road; tel: 6385 8752; www.crystaljade.com; daily 11am–3pm, 5–11.30pm; $$; Metro: Line 1, Huangpi; map p.138 A4

This upscale eatery represents the latest trend in Shanghai dining: a mix of Shanghai and Cantonese offerings served in an upscale setting. Try the steamed pork dumplings, *dan dan mian* (spicy noodles in peanut sauce) or stir-fried southern vegetables.

Din Tai Fung

2/F, Unit 11A South Block Plaza,

Shanghai excels in **food delivery**, and the Sherpa company (www.sherpa.com.cn; tel: 6209 6209) employs a fleet of scooters that delivers food throughout the city, at all hours, for Rmb15–35. Sherpa works with more than 100 restaurants; call Sherpa, not the restaurants. Some restaurants have their own delivery service as well.

123 Xingye Road; tel: 6385 8378; www.dintaifung.com.tw; Mon–Thur 11am–3pm, 5pm–midnight, Fri 11am–3pm, 5pm–1am, Sat–Sun 11am–1am; $$; Metro: Line 1, Huangpi; map p.138 A4

This Taiwanese chain knows its steamed dumplings, and the perpetual long line-ups guarantee just-cooked freshness. It features a large glass viewing window, where you can watch the cooks roll, cut, fill and steam a delicious assortment of dumplings. The house special is *xiao long bao* – steamed dumplings filled with pork, ginger, garlic, scallions and a scalding hot broth.

The Fat Olive

6/F, Silver Court Building, 228 Xizang Road South, near Huaihai East Road; tel: 6334 3288; www.thefatolive.com; 9.30am– 10.30pm, bar open late; $$; Metro: Line 8, Dashijie; Bus: 17, 3, 42; map p.134 B1

The latest venue from Australian chef David Laris features Greek *mezedes*, or snack food, and the fine small pizzas, lamb kebabs, pitta bread, feta cheese rolled in grape leaves and similar fare are accompanied by a simple wine list. Try to book a seat outside during nice weather; they fill up fast.

Soahc

Bldg 3, South Block, Lane 123, Xingye Road, near Huangpi South Road; tel: 6385 7777; daily 10am–10pm; $$; Metro: Line 1, Huangpi; map p.138 A4

Taiwanese owner Lily Ho was once a famous Hong Kong movie star, who later resurfaced as a restaurateur with this beautifully designed venue. Specialities include an exceptional,

Left: Nan Xiang. **Above:** New Heights *(see p.101)*.

melt-in-your mouth lion's-head meatball with crab meat, while the lotus root appetiser and the subtly spicy Sichuan smoked duck are also superb.

Urban Soup Kitchen

280 Madang Road, near Zizhong Road; tel: 5382 2978; www. urbansoupkitchen.com; daily 10am–10pm; $; Metro: Line 1, Huangpi; map p.138 A4

This unpretentious place serves the best soup and sandwiches in town, which is not an easy feat. The formula is simple – fresh ingredients, no preservatives – and they deliver, too, if you get hungry in your hotel room.

Xin Ji Shi

Bldg 9, North Block, Lane 123, Xingye Road; tel: 6336 4746; daily 10am–11pm; $$; Metro: Line 1, Huangpi; map p.138 A4

A big, popular and very good Shanghainese restaurant in Xintiandi that serves reliable versions of all the local classics: rich stewed pork ribs, crab-egg tofu, lion's-head meatballs, and the rest, along with some of the best tea in town.

Ye Shanghai

Bldg 6, North Block, Lane 123, Xingye Road; tel: 6311 2323; www.elite-concepts.com/ yeshanghai; daily 11.30am– 2.30pm, 6–10.30pm; $$; Metro: Line 1, Huangpi; map p.138 A4

Sit upstairs where the ceilings are higher, and soak in the 'old Shanghai' atmosphere, along with a lighter, less oily take on some of the classics of local cuisine: try the stir-fried shrimp in longjing tea leaves.

Hongkou and Suzhou Creek

d.g.b Restaurant & Lounge

130 Yichang Road, near Jiang Ning Road; tel: 5155 8311; Mon–Fri 2.30pm–1.30am, Sat–Sun 11.30am–11pm; $$; Metro: Line 4, Zhenping, then taxi

Come here for a look at the László Hudec-designed Art Deco brewery on the banks of Suzhou Creek, which has been converted into this huge-but-intimate dining environment. It serves traditional French cuisine, with a modern approach.

The Factory

1/F, Bldg 4, 29 Shajing Road, in the 1933 Old Millfun Complex;

103

If you are stuck for dining options, go to Xintiandi. The restaurants tend to be more expensive than their counterparts in the old French Concession, but there are reasonable outlets alongside the expensive ones. It has a wide range of options, and the open-air, pedestrian-only layout is perfect for browsing.

tel: 6563 3393; www.factory shanghai.com; Mon–Fri 2.30pm–1.30am, Sat–Sun 11.30am–11pm; $$; Metro: Line 4, Hailun, then 10-minute walk

The Factory is in the spectacular converted warehouse of the 1933 complex, where it serves a bright, modern menu that effortlessly mixes East and West. But in the end, the setting, not the food, is the star of this show.

Nanjing Road West Area

Gourmet Café

455 Shaanxi Road North; tel: 5213 6885; www.gourmet-café.com; Mon–Fri 11.30am–2.30pm, 6.30–11pm, Sat–Sun 11.30am–11pm; $$; Metro: Line 2, Nanjing West, then 5-minute taxi; map p.133 C2

This cosy little café has found a niche: it serves the best hamburgers and french fries in town. They make 30 kinds of hamburgers, and they grind their own beef as well, so don't be afraid to order yours medium-rare.

Qimin Organic Hot Pot

407 Shaanxi North Road, by Beijing West Road; tel: 6258 8777; www.qi-min.com/shanghai-eng/main.html; noon–10pm; $$; Metro: Line 2, Nanjing West; map p.133 C2

Ambience is not usually associated with hotpot restaurants, but this place is a happy exception. In addition to sourcing organic ingredients for the menu, the Taiwanese owners take special care to make sure the broths are superb and not flavoured with MSG. And since you cook the meal yourself, there's no quibbling with the chef over technique. Reservations recommended.

Spice Spirit

7/F, Westgate Mall, 1038 Nanjing Road West; tel: 6217 1777; 11am–10pm; Metro: Line 2, Nanjing West Road; map p.133 D2

It claims to serve the spiciest food in town, and who could argue? The hotpot is a volcanic brew of red-hot Sichuan pepper, chilli, garlic, shallots and stock that will have you crying for a cold *pijiu* (beer).

Former French Concession North

Cantina Agave

291 Fumin Road and Changle Road; tel: 6170 1310; www.cantinaagave.com; daily 11am–11pm; $$; Metro: Line 1, Changshu; map p.137 C4

Cantina Agave opened with a bang in 2009, and its indoor-outdoor seating, excellent Mexican food – light tacos, burritos, chicken mole, nachos and so on – and generous margaritas made it an instant hit. Reservations are recommended.

Casa 13

House 13, 1100 Huashan Road, by Xinguo Road; tel: 5238 2782;

www.casa13.cn; Tue–Sat
11am–11pm, Sun 11am–5pm;
$$$; Metro: Line 1, Changshu,
then taxi; map p.136 A3
Located in a lane-house far
from the busy Shanghai
streets, this intimate restaurant offers a relaxing atmosphere with a greenhouse and
patio as well as a main dining
room and bar. Menu highlights include the warm
Camembert and pate platter,
the beef cheeks and the osso
bucco.

Charmant

1418 Huaihai Road Central, near
Fuxing Road Central; tel: 6431
8107/6431 8027; daily 11–4am;
$$; Metro: Line 1, Changshu;
map p.136 C3
This family-style restaurant
stays open late, and serves
Taiwanese comfort food,
such as oysters in black bean
and scallion, taro cakes,
spicy pork with young bamboo shoots, in a city-centre
location. You know it's good,
because it is popular with
Taiwanese diners, who are
famously finicky about their
food.

Chun Kitchen

124 Jinxian Road, near the corner of Maoming Road South; tel:
6256 0301; daily 6pm and 8pm
seatings; $–$$; Metro: Line 1,
Shaanxi; map p.137 D4
Chun is like eating in the
home of a fussy but friendly
Chinese grandmother: it has
four tiny tables, and you eat
what the owner, Ms Qu, has
bought fresh in the market
that day. The offerings are
sweet, heavy, oily and
unapologetically Shanghainese, such as snails, eels,
fish and pork ribs. There are
two evening seatings, and
reservations are required.

Franck

376 Wukang Road, Ferguson
Lane; tel: 6437 6465; www.
franck.com.cn; noon–2.30pm,
7–10.30pm, closed Sun night,
Mon, Tue lunch; $$–$$$;
Metro: Line 1, Changshu; map
p.136 B2
French brasserie cuisine,
such as beef tartare, confit
de canard and roast chicken,
that is beautifully executed
and served in a casual-chic
space complete with brusque
French-speaking waiting
staff. Ultra-popular with
Shanghai expats.

A Future Perfect

No. 16, Lane 351, Hua Shan
Road, near Changle Road; tel:
6248 8020; www.afuture
perfect.com.cn; Tue–Sun
11am–11pm; $$; Metro: Line 2,
Jing'an Temple, then taxi; map
p.136 B3
This tucked-away little gem is
not easy to find: at the end of
a little lane lies a semi-bohemian restaurant in a
lovely concession-era villa.
The menu is Continental, the
breakfasts are excellent, the
patio is intimate and tree-lined, and the bread is the
best in town.

Guyi Hunan

87 Fumin Road, near Ju Lu
Road; tel: 6249 5628; daily
11am–2pm, 5.30–10.30pm; $$;

> Price for a two-course dinner
> per person, with one drink:
> $ less than $15
> $$ $15–30
> $$$ $30–60
> $$$$ more than $60

Metro: Line 2, Jinan Temple,
then taxi; map p.136 C4
This sparkling little restaurant, with its monumentally
spicy food, is a good place
for a lively, peppery, let-your-hair-down dinner. Hunan cuisine is similar to Sichuan, but
the offerings at Guyi are more
refined, less oily and garlicky
and soupy, than most of the
city's spicy offerings.

La Grange

794 Ju Lu Road, near Fumin
Road; tel: 6248 2185;
www.lagrange.asia; Mon–Sat
11.30am–2.30pm, 6.30–
10.30pm; $$$$; Metro: Line 2,
Jing'an Temple, then taxi; map
p.136 C4
With its boutique atmosphere, impressive wine list
and resolutely French menu,
La Grange brings a touch of
Paris into the old French
Concession. The menu is
southwestern French, with a
variety of braised and slow-cooked specialties, and La
Grange is a smart alternative
to the better-known restaurants on the Bund.

Left: Kathleen's 5 *(see p.102).*
Right: A Future Perfect.

105

Little Face

30 Donghu Road, near Huaihai Middle Road; tel: 6466 4328; www.facebars.com; daily 11am–2.30pm, 5.30–10.30pm; $$$; Metro: Line 1, Changshu; map p.137 C4

A firm favourite with residents, this little eatery serves pan-Asian food, including Thai, Chinese and Southeast Asian curries, spring rolls, papaya salads and grilled beef, in an old Shanghai atmosphere filled with antique furniture.

Lost Heaven Yunnan

38 Gao You Road, near Fuxing West Road; tel: 6433 5126; www.lostheaven.com.cn; daily 11am–2pm, 5.30–10.30pm; $$; Metro: Line 1, Changshu, then taxi; map p.136 B3

Owner Robin Yin travels frequently to Yunnan province in search of authentic native ingredients, and the menu

Price for a two-course dinner per person, with one drink:
$ less than $15
$$ $15–30
$$$ $30–60
$$$$ more than $60

features exotic mushrooms, vegetables, spices and preparations that can't be found anywhere else. The design is dazzling as well; don't miss the two-storey wall made from blocks of pu'er tea.

Maya

No. 2 Bldg, 568 Ju Lu Road, inside the Shanghai Grand Plaza compound; tel: 6289 6889; www.cosmogroup. cn/maya; daily 5pm–1am, brunch Sat–Sun 11am–5pm; $$$; Metro: Line 1, Shaanxi; map p.137 D4

This tucked-away Mexican restaurant serves creative versions of time-honoured south-of-the-border favourites, such as lime beef, cilantro chicken and a number of good fish dishes, along with generous jugs of sangria.

Mesa Restaurant

748 Ju Lu Road, between Fumin and Xiangyang North roads; tel: 6289 9108; www.mesa-manifesto.com; daily 11am–2pm, 6–11pm, Sat–Sun 9.30–5pm; $$$; Metro: Line 2, Jing'an Temple, then taxi; map p.137 C4

Mesa Restaurant is a time-honoured Western food favourite in an old electronics warehouse. It smacks of modern Shanghai, from its central location and sunny terrace right down to the beautiful black-clad waiting staff. Try the lamb chops, or, if you book early, the ever-popular Sunday brunch.

Otto Restaurant and Wine Bar

85 Fumin Road, near Ju Lu Road; tel: 6248 9186; www.otto-café.com; 10.30am–10pm; $$; Metro: Line 2, Jing'an Temple, then taxi; map p.136 C4

With communal tables next to picture windows, Otto offers a convivial and lively atmosphere. Italian fare is varied and well done, but the highlight of this venue is the large range of wines available by the glass. Dozens of bottles are sealed in specially designed cases that allow sampling without damaging the wine that remains in the bottle.

Oyama

2/F, 20 Donghu Road, near Huaihai Middle Road; tel: 5404 7705;

Mon–Sat 5.30–10.30pm; $$$$; Metro: Line 1, Shaanxi; map p.137 C4

This 14-seat, reservations-only restaurant offers a custom menu that changes nightly, depending on which ingredients the eponymous master chef imports fresh from Japan that day. It features the best sushi this side of Japan, and melt-in-your-mouth kobe beef, along with a handsome selection of fine sakes. Reservations required.

People 7

805 Ju Lu Road, near Fumin Road; tel: 5404 0707; daily 11.30am–2pm, 6pm–midnight; $$; Metro: Line 2, Jing'an Temple, then taxi; map p.136 C4

There is no sign out front, and you have to 'know' how to open the door, which is annoying, but once inside, this cavernous industrial-style space, with its blue-neon bar, dim spotlighting, and contemporary pan-Chinese cuisine, is worth the effort.

Left: Casa 13 (see p.104). **Right and above:** Lost Heaven on the Bund (see p.100).

Quan Ju De

4/F, 786 Huaihai Road Central, near Ruijin Road; tel: 5404 5799; www.quanjude.com.cn; daily 11am–10.30pm; $$; Metro: Line 1, Shaanxi; map p.137 E4

If spicy Sichuan food is not your cup of chilli oil, then try the northern-style roast duck at this popular branch of the famous Beijing duck chain. The duck skin is crispy, the pancakes are fresh, and the dipping sauce is a closely guarded secret. The restaurant chain was originally established in Beijing in 1894, so they've had time to perfect their technique.

Shintori

803 Ju Lu Road, near Fumin Road; tel: 5404 5252; Mon–Fri 5.30–11pm, Sat–Sun 11.30am–2pm, 5–11pm; $$$; Metro: Line 2, Jing'an Temple, then taxi; map p.136 C4

Shintori has a lovely, bamboo-bedecked sidewalk entrance that leads to a large, open dining room featuring a subtle, minimalist design and high ceilings, along with an open kitchen that turns out a fine selection of sushi and sashimi, along

with updated versions of other Japanese classics.

South Beauty 881

881 Central Yan An Road; tel: 6247 6682; http://southbeauty group.com/en; daily 10.30am–11.30pm, bar until 2am; $$–$$$; Metro: Line 1, Shaanxi or Jing'an Temple; map p.133 C1

This impressive venue serves first-rate Sichuan food in a century-old mansion and grounds that have been converted into a state-of-the-art modern restaurant. The food is genuine, tongue-searing Sichuan that'll make you reach for a cold drink; the signature dish

Left: Mesa Restaurant (*see p.106*).

Hengshan Café

308 Hengshan Road, by Gao'an Road; tel: 6471 7127; daily 10.30–3.30am; $; Metro: Line 1, Hengshan; map p.136 B2

This clean, well-lit café features a light, friendly selection of Cantonese and Shanghainese dishes. Start with some barbecue pork or roast duck, and continue with the 'tiger-striped' chilli peppers, stewed ribs, steamed fish and crispy stir-fried vegetables. Make a reservation.

Jesse Restaurant

41 Tian Ping Road, near Huaihai Middle Road; tel: 6282 9260; daily 11am–midnight; $$; Metro: Line 1, Hengshan, then taxi; map p.136 B2

This charming hole in the wall serves some of the tastiest Shanghainese food in town – red-cooked pork ribs, stir-fried vegetables, steamed fish – as evidenced by the clusters of hungry people waiting outside. It is small, plain and unpretentious, but it really is one of the best.

is beef cooked at the table in hot spicy oil.

Southern Barbarian

Area E, 2/F, Ju Roshine Life Art Space, 56 Maoming South Road, near Changle Road; tel: 5157 5510; www.southernbarbarian.com.cn; daily 10am–10pm; $–$$; Metro: Line 1, Shaanxi; map p.137 D4

Yunnanese cuisine is typified by ingredients like cheese, whole cooked beans and exotic mushrooms, and Southern Barbarian serves some of the best. Try the jizhong mushrooms, the fried goat's-milk cheese, or the clay-pot chicken – you won't be disappointed.

Wan Chai

858 Ju Lu Road, near Changshu Road; tel: 6248 5992; daily 11am–10pm; $; Metro: Line 1, Changshu; map p.136 C4

Good Cantonese food is rare in Shanghai, but Wan Chai delivers reliable versions of southern favourites like camphor duck, steamed fish, barbecue chicken dipped in salt and black pepper, and fresh prawns stir-fried in rock salt, garlic and chilli.

Former French Concession South

Haiku by Hatsune

28B Taojiang Road, by Hengshan Road; tel: 6445 0021; daily 11.30am–2pm, 5.30–10pm, Fri–Sat until 11pm; $$–$$$; Metro: Line 1, between Changshu and Hengshan; map p.136 C2

The Japanese fusion treats and cutting-edge decor of Haiku are perfect for a friendly, boisterous meal after a long day out. It sits on one of the old Concession's most charming streets, surrounded by a wealth of after-dinner drinking options, and its fusion-inspired sushi is bold and original.

Qian Qui Shan Fang

15 Baoqing Road, near Fuxing Road; tel: 6437 7597; daily 8am–3am; $; Metro: Line 1, Changshu; map p.137 C3

Qian Qui serves steamed buns, stir-fried vegetables and meat, cold appetisers, and other family-style Shanghai favourites in a clean, bright, café-style restaurant that features good service and low prices. The savoury pancake rolled with beef slices and cucumbers, and the chicken soup noodles, are among the favourites. Perfect for a quick, inexpensive lunch or dinner.

> Price for a two-course dinner per person, with one drink:
> $ less than $15
> $$ $15–30
> $$$ $30–60
> $$$$ more than $60

In most cases, local chain restaurants in Shanghai vary widely in quality. For example, there are two branches of the Hunan restaurant Di Shui Dong, but the outlet on Maoming Road is infinitely better. The same applies to Shanghainese chain Xinjishi: the outlet on Taojiang Road is insipid and overpriced, while the same restaurant in Xintiandi is excellent. The one exception is Spicy-Joint, the fast-expanding Sichuan chain, where all the locations are equally good.

South Beauty

28 Taojiang Road, by Baoqing Road; tel: 6445 2581/6445 2582; http://southbeauty group.com; daily 10.30am–midnight; $$–$$$; Metro: Line 1, Changshu; map p.136 C2

It has Zen-style minimalist decor, the waiting staff wear classy uniforms, and it costs more than most Sichuan restaurants in town, but the food at South Beauty is exceptional: the fish is fresh, the beef tender and the vegetables crisp and flavourful. Reservations are recommended.

Vargas Grill

3/F, 18 Dongping Road, between Wulumuqi and Hengshan Roads; tel: 6437 0136; www.vargusgrill. com; daily 11am–2.30pm, 5.30–10.30pm; $$; Metro: Line 1, between Changshu and Hengshan; map p.136 C3

Meat is the star of this show, as the latest venue opened by fast-rising local chef Eduardo Vargas specialises in char-grilled steaks and chops, and ribs flavoured by a tasty variety of rubs, sauces and marinades. If that is not sufficient, you can top it off with one of Eduardo's rich, buttery desserts.

Vedas

550 Jian Guo Road West, near Wulumuqi Road; tel: 6445 8100; www.vedascuisine.com; daily 11.30am–2.30, 5.30–11pm; $$; Metro: Line 1, Hengshan; map p.137 C2

Right: Shintori *(see p.107).*

The best Indian restaurant in town, Vedas combines an open kitchen, classy but understated decor and refined versions of many Indian classics, with the Bombay prawn curry and tandoori chicken among the highlights.

Western Shanghai

Ba Guo Bu Yi
1018 Dingxi Road, near Yan'an Road West; tel: 5239 7779; www.baguobuyi.com; daily 11am–2pm, 5–10pm; $; Metro: Lines 3, 4, West Yan'an

This restaurant is loved for its low prices and its *re nao* (hot and noisy) atmosphere. The food is authentic Sichuan, featuring red-hot pots of beef and fish soaking in a fiery stew of chilli-peppered and garlicky glory.

Dong Bei Ren
46 Panyu Road, near Yan'an

Price for a two-course dinner per person, with one drink:
$ less than $15
$$ $15–30
$$$ $30–60
$$$$ more than $60

Road West; tel: 5230 2230; daily 10am–10pm; $; Bus: 71, 76, 925; map p.136 A3

Expect colourful uniforms, singing staff and over-the-top decor, along with rich and hearty meat-and-potatoes cuisine, and Harbin beer that is plentiful and cheap. Eat the potatoes with green peppers and eggplant, or the lamb dumplings, or, if you dare, don a pair of clear plastic gloves and pick up a piece of roasted lamb shank.

Lao Tan Guizhou
2/F, 42 Xingfu Road, near Fa Hua Zhen Road; tel: 6283 7843; daily 11am–10.30pm; $; Metro: Lines 3, 4, West Yan'an; map p.136 A2

Lao Tan features the smoky homemade hams and bacons of Guizhou province. The signature dish is *la zi ji*, or spicy chicken, but it is braised, not fried as it is in Sichuan cuisine, so it is more tender and juicy.

Matsuri 123
4/F, 951 Hong Xu Road, on the corner of Yan'an Road West; tel: 6262 7123; www.matsuri-123.com; Mon–Fri 5–11pm, Sat–Sun 11am–3pm, 5–11pm;

$$; Metro: Line 1, Loushanguan, then 10-minute taxi; Bus: 69, 748, 925

Matsuri means festival in Japanese, and this place is a full-on party, a giant all-you-can-eat Japanese smorgasbord filled with food stations serving yakitori, teppanyaki, sushi and sashimi, eel rice, miso soup, desserts and more, along with a free flow of sake and beer.

Old Station
201 Caoxi Road North, near Nan Dan Road; tel: 6427 2233; daily 11am–2pm, 5.30–10pm; $$; Metro: Line 1, Xujiahui

Only in Shanghai, perhaps, could a former French nunnery be converted into a museum-restaurant filled with old train carriages, in which you can dine. The food is classic Shanghainese, with sautéed fresh shrimp, lion's-head meatballs, stewed pork ribs, and fried and steamed fish from the nearby shallow seas.

Xin Jiang Style Restaurant
280 Yi Shan Road, near Nan Dan Road; tel: 6468 9198; daily

10am–2am; $; Metro: Lines 3, 4, Yi Shan

Xinjiang food, from the Muslim far west of China, features hearty lamb and chicken and potato dishes, along with the famous home-made flatbread. The roast lamb is expertly cooked, moist and lean and falling off the bone. Natives of the province swear that this is the best Xinjiang restaurant in town.

Pudong

The Kitchen Salvatore Cuomo

2967 Binjiang Dadao, near Fenghe Road, Pudong Riverfront; tel: 5054 1265; daily 11am–2.30pm, 6–10pm; $$; Metro: Line 2, Lujiazui; map p.135 D4

Left: South Beauty *(see p.107)*.
Above: views of Pudong.

The good news is there is no **tipping** in Shanghai, none at all, so don't ever do it. The bad news comes in the form of a 10–15% service charge that is levied by some – but not all – restaurants. Check the fine print at the bottom of the menu to avoid an unpleasant shock when the bill arrives.

A favourite among Italians living in Shanghai as well as those who enjoy simple yet delicious Italian dishes. Set against the waterfront under the Oriental Pearl Tower, this venue offers good views along with its pizza and perfectly cooked pasta dishes.

Sushi Inc

33 Huayuanshiqiao, 2/F Citigroup Tower, near Fucheng Road; tel: 5877 6551; daily 11am–2.30pm, 5–9.30pm;

$–$$; Metro: Line 2, Lujiazui; map p.135 D3

This Californian-style Japanese restaurant is managed by the same people who launched the cult-worthy Haiku by Hatsune. Menu items include a different range of nigiri sushi, as well as a yakitori selection.

Y's Table

B/2 World Financial Centre, 100 Century Boulevard, near Dongtai Road; tel: 6877 6865; daily 10am–10pm; $; Metro: Line 2, Lujiazui; map p.135 E3

Located at the bottom of the tallest building in the city, this giant 514-seat restaurant is an elevated version of a food fair that allows groups of people to enjoy dishes from different cooking stations hosted by top local restaurants.

111

Shopping

Nanjing West and Huaihai roads are the king and queen of Shanghai shopping, respectively, but other neighbourhoods offer a diversity not found in the chain outlets. The malls and small shops of Xujiahui bring out the daily crowds, while the boutiques along Changle, Xinle and Shaanxi roads are on the browsing routes of the city's fashionistas. Meanwhile, Taikang Road and Yuyuan Bazaar both offer a staggering variety of kitschy and creative finds. Other neighbourhoods, like the stretch along Fumin and Julu roads, as well as the area around Jing 'An Temple, are rife with window-shopping opportunities.

Antiques

Brocade Country

616 Julu Road, near Xiangyang Road; daily 10.30am–7pm; tel: 6279 2677; Metro: Line 1, Shaanxi; Bus: 48, 94; map p.133 C1

Liu Xiao Lan has for years collected interesting custom-made clothing and antique textiles handmade by ethnic minorities from the southwest of China. Xiao Lan speaks impeccable English and can tell the stories behind the pieces.

Chine Antique

1665 Hongqiao Road, near Shuicheng Road; tel: 6270 1023; daily 10am–7pm; Metro: Line 2, Loushanguan, then taxi

Chine specialises in wooden antique furniture and offers overseas shipping services. English-speaking staff are knowledgeable. Located in Hongqiao in the western part of the city.

Dongtai Road Antiques Market

175 Dongtai Road, between Chongde and Xizang Roads; daily 9am–6pm; Metro: Line 1,

Antique items that are more than 200 years old are not permitted to leave the country, but few things in antique markets are actually that old. Art Deco lamps and furniture are very popular, and therefore prices have increased dramatically in recent years. Beware of 'faked' antiques, which are new items made to look authentically old; often, what looks like a centuries-old patina is simply a handful of mud rubbed on a couple of weeks ago. Having said that, Shanghai is the best place in China to buy genuine antiques, because traders from around China bring their wares here, where asking prices are the highest.

between Huangpi and People's Square; Bus: 17, 581, 864; map p.138 B4

Although this market offers few authentic antiques, it does have its genuine gems, and serious searchers can find Art Deco period pieces in the surrounding lanes. Much of it, though, is tacky Mao memorabilia, porcelain ware, coins, carv-

ings and other modern China gewgaws.

Fuyou Road Antique Market

459 Fangbang Middle Road, in the Yuyuan Bazaar area; Mon–Fri 9am–5pm, Sat–Sun 5am–5pm; Bus: 64, 926, 945; map p.134 C1

Die-hard enthusiasts get here at the crack of dawn with flashlights in hand to steal a march on the crowds that form, especially on Sunday mornings when people from the countryside come to town with their wares. This is a mix of flea market and junk yard, but there are genuine treasures here.

Henry Antique Warehouse

3/F, Bldg 2, 361 Hongzhong Road, near Hechuanzhi 2nd Road; tel: 6401 0831; daily 9am–6pm; www.h-antique.com; Bus: 804

Located in the western reaches of Shanghai's Hongqiao area, this warehouse is filled with antique furniture such as tables, chairs, screens, armoires and more. Most of them are from

Left: Hongqiao Flower Market. **Below:** malls dominate the new Shanghai.

the top floor and a supermarket and food fair on the basement level.

Plaza 66

1266 Nanjing Road West, by Shaanxi Road; tel: 6279 0910; daily 10am–10pm; Metro: Line 2, Nanjing West; Bus: 24, 738, 955; map p.133 C2

Best known for its top-end designer brand stores such as Fendi, Lagerfeld and Christian Dior, Plaza 66 is home to some of the most prestigious retail space in the city, but because of the hefty luxury tax, this mall is largely left to the window-shoppers.

Raffles City

268 Xizhang Middle Road; tel: 6340 3600; daily 10am–10pm; Metro: Lines 1, 2, 8, People's Park; map p.134 A3

This slice of Singapore is popular with the young and the trendy, as well as nearby office workers. In addition to funky fashions, Raffles City also features a cinema, scores of restaurants on the upper floors and a busy food fair in the basement that connects to the Metro station.

At markets where many vendors sell the same item, **bargaining** is completely acceptable. Don't be afraid to argue down the asking price (cut by half or more at most places), and make concessions towards the middle ground. Often, if you walk away in the midst of negotiations, the vendor will chase after you offering an astoundingly low price.

---

the post-1911 era, but there are a few older Qing-Dynasty pieces.

Malls

Grand Gateway

1 Hongqiao Road, by Zhaojiabang Road; tel: 6407 0111; daily 10am–10pm; Metro: Line 1, Xujiahui

Situated at the base of two prominent lipstick-shaped towers in the heart of Xujiahui's commercial district, the Grand Gateway is the largest shopping mall on the Puxi side. The retail mix ranges from high-end on the first two levels to mid-range in the upper levels, with restaurants and a cinema on

Super Brand Mall

168 Lujiazui West Road, by Yincheng West Road; tel: 6887 7888; www.superbrandmall.com; daily 10am–10pm; Metro: Line 2, Lujiazui; map p135 D3

Super Brand Mall was billed as Shanghai's largest mall in 2002 when it first opened, and has managed to retain this title. It recently underwent a major renovation and has emerged with a new retail mix that includes Zara, H&M, Sephora, Nike, Toys R Us and the ultra-popular Japanese outlets of Uniqlo and Muji. It also features one of the city's few ice-skating rinks.

Times Square

99 Huaihai Middle Road; tel: 6391 0691; www.shtimes square.com; daily 10am–10pm; Metro: Line 1, Huangpi; Bus: 920, 926, 983; map p.134 B4

Attracting a more fashion-conscious crowd than most malls, Shanghai Times Square occasionally features art exhibits and short classical concerts on Friday evenings. Outlets include Coach, Bally,

> A 30% tax is levied on **luxury goods** in China, which is why many wealthy consumers prefer to go to Hong Kong or Macau for their luxury goods shopping sprees.

Givenchy, Gucci and Max Mara, as well as Chaterhouse bookstore and City Shop, a pricey grocery store specialising in imported goods.

Westgate Mall

1038 Nanjing Road West; tel: 6218 7878; www.westgate mall.com.cn; daily 10am–10pm; Metro: Line 2, Nanjing West Station; Bus: 24, 738, 955; map p.133 D2

Anchored by the upscale Japanese department store Isetan, this mall is distinguished by its expansive open first floor, which is often used for exhibitions and promotional events. Prestigious brand-name outlets such as Burberry and Givenchy lend class, while the innovative food court and supermarket in the basement level draw the crowds.

Markets

Hongqiao Flower Market

718 Hongjing Road, south of Yan'an West Road; tel: 5117 3882; daily 8am–6pm; Metro: Line 2, Loushanguan, then taxi: Bus: 721, 809, 936

In addition to featuring an enormous collection of indoor and outdoor plants and cut flowers, this market also has a number of vendors specialising in housewares and home decor.

Longhua Fashion and Gift Market

2465 Longhua Road, near Huarong Road; Metro: Line 4, Shanghai Stadium

This is one of two destinations where vendors have relocated since the infamous Xiangyang Market (better known as the fakes market) was closed down in 2006, the other being the Yatai Market in the Shanghai Science Museum Metro station. Clothing, shoes, housewares, electronics and toys fill the 600 stalls on three floors – this is the best place to buy those fakes.

Nihong Kids Plaza, also known as Pu'an Lu Children's Market

10 Pu'an Road, near Jinlin Middle Road, basement level; tel: 5383 6218; daily 9.30am–8pm; Metro: Line 1, Huangpu Road; map p.134 A2

Dozens of stalls sell a trove of young children's and infant clothing, shoes and cheap plastic toys, in international brands such as Carters,

Gymboree and Circo. Bargaining will probably only get you a few Rmb off the asking price, but prices are generally reasonable.

Qipu Wholesale Market

168 Qipu Road, near Henan Road; daily 9am–5pm; Metro: Line 3, Baoshan; Bus: 724

Four main buildings in this area are crammed with stalls selling mostly women's fashions and accessories. Qipu, pronounced 'cheap-u', is only for the brave of heart: it is extremely crowded, chaotic, and is filled with aggressive touts and pickpockets. But the payoffs for the hard bargainer are unbeatable prices.

Shanghai Cybermart

1 Huaihai East Road, near Xizang Road; daily 10am–8pm; Metro: Line 8, Dashijie; map p.134 B2

Three storeys of consumer electronics are for sale here. Brand-name goods have a

duty imposed upon them, so the best prices may not be very low, but accessories such as memory sticks and external drives can be had for a bargain.

Shanghai Sanyeh Wholesale Market

Moling Road, 5/F, Huanlong Shopping Centre, Shanghai Railway Station South Square; daily 8.30am–7.30pm; Metro: Line 1, Shanghai Train Station, exit 4

Leave the Metro station via exit 4 and turn right to find the Huanlong Shopping Centre. On the fifth floor, dozens of stalls sell eyeglass frames and sunglasses, and they will also test your eyes and fill the

Left: a traditional cloth market. **Above:** fresh fish at a wet market.

The first rule of **bargaining** is don't offer a price unless you intend to purchase the item, so it is wise to check out the item first to determine its value. You will be yelled at if you walk away after a vendor has agreed to your price, but of course, refusing to buy is your prerogative.

115

prescription while you wait. Generic and brand-name frames are on sale here, and vigorous bargaining will get you a pair for about Rmb200.

Shiliu Puhong Qixiang Cloth Market

168 Dongmen Road; tel: 6330 1043; daily 10am–6pm; Bus: 64, 43, 89; map p.135 D1

When the old fabric market on Dongjiadu Road was shut down, vendors moved to one of two nearby locations. This one is located between Yuyuan Garden and the South Bund. It features scores of fabric vendors on three floors where you can have clothing made to measure or bring favourite items of clothing to be copied. Tailoring tends to take three to five days. Be sure to leave time in case the first fitting proves unsuccessful.

South Bund Fabric Market

399 Lujiabang Road; tel: 6377 2236; daily 10am–7pm; Metro: Line 4, Nanpu Bridge; Bus: 43, 64, 931; map p.138 B3

As with the above fabric market, this features three floors of fabric vendors with tailor-

> Beware of **pickpockets** and keep an eye on your valuables at all times. Markets where domestic and local tourists congregate tend to be easy pickings for thieves, whose audacity makes up for what is sometimes a very comical lack of skill.

ing services. This one is more popular among foreigners living in Shanghai, but both seem comparable in the kinds of fabrics and services available. Although tailoring quality may vary from stall to stall, some recommendations include stalls 130 and 135 for suits, 282 for cashmere, wool and leather coats and jackets, and 264 for traditional Chinese wear.

Tongchuan Fish Market

800 Tongchuan Road, near Caoyang Road; daily 6.30am–5pm; Metro: Line 4, Caoyang, then taxi

Buckets of fresh and freshly frozen seafood items can be bought and taken to nearby restaurants, where they will cook up your purchases for a fee (usually Rmb10 per catty

for fish and less for shellfish). Bargaining is a must, especially for the local delicacy, hairy crab, which is in season from October to December.

Yatai Market

Daily 10am–9pm; Metro: Line 2, Shanghai Science and Technology Museum

Dozens of vendors have set up shop within the station selling knock-off branded goods and other generic items that range from suitcases to scarves. Aggressive bargaining is advised.

Yuyuan Bazaar

Fuyou Road and Jiujiachang Road; daily 8.30am–8.30pm; Metro: Line 8, Laoximen, then taxi; Bus: 932; map p.135 C2

Surrounding the bustling Yuyuan Garden are stores selling souvenirs, such as T-shirts, silk robes and tea. But in the outlying areas beyond the garden are non-descript buildings where you can buy all manner of odds and ends such as chopsticks, umbrellas, toys, plastic items and Chinese chess and mah-jong sets. As always, bargain hard.

Shopping Neighbourhoods

Nanjing Road has been Shanghai's premier shopping street for decades. It is home to the famous old **Shanghai Number One Department Store** on the corner of Nanjing East Road and Xizhang Road, which for years was the only venue where foreign goods could be purchased. Today, the street is open to pedestrians only and features scores of international as well as local-brand stores. Further west, Nanjing moves dramatically upscale, selling the world's top luxury brands in world-class shopping malls.

There are other shopping streets as well: **Fuzhou Road**, which runs east to west between the Bund and People's Park, is known for its bookstores, stationery and art supply stores, while Guangdong Road near Yunnan Road has a number of beauty salon supply stores selling hair products and styling

Left and above: Huaihai Road. **Right:** Nanjing Road East.

The Expat Learning Centre offers the **Bargain Hunters Shopping Tour**, a full-day tour of Shanghai's shopping highlights with lessons on bargaining, assessing the value of goods and other shopping tips for US$100 (www.shanghai-classes.com; tel: 5588 9133).

tools, nail polish, spa treatment packages and wigs.

Taikang Road, or Tian Zi Fang

Unlike the more polished Xintiandi, this collection of galleries, retail outlets, bars and restaurants within the narrow alleyways of Taikang Road is a result of organic growth rather than calculated planning, and the result is conducive to hours of browsing, nibbling and imbibing. The starting point is fairly easy to find, at Lane 210 on Taikang Road between Sinan and Ruijin roads.

Look for the **Pottery Workshop** with its hand-thrown cups, teapots and other ceramic collectables. Straight ahead on the right at

No. 3 is the **International Artist Factory**, home to **NEST** on the third floor, a collection of products by local expats who are committed to environmentally sustainable businesses.

Further along the strip are **Marion Carsten**, who specialises in tasteful yet interesting silver jewellery, **Julia Koo**, who creates luxurious silk kimonos and dresses, **Zakku**, a collection of Vietnamese housewares and accessories, and **Feel Shanghai**, known for its traditional Chinese costumes. Turn left further on and continue past the covered well and follow the twists and turns to **Lane 247**, where a cluster

cashmere with modern Asian influences. The silk embroidered mobile phone holders and cashmere blankets lined with silk are among the many highlights.

Feine, Shanghai
392 Wukang Road, near Xingguo and Huaihai Middle Roads; tel: 6437 3835; www.feine shanghai.com; daily 10am–7pm; Metro: Line 1, Hengshan; map p.136 B3

Newly opened by the husband-and-wife team of Anja and Ashley Jones, Feine offers a range of cashmere clothing and accessories for men, women and children.

Lilli's Shanghai
Main showroom: Maosheng Mansion, 1D, 1051 Xinzha Road, near Xikang Road; tel: 6215 5031; www.lillishanghai.com; Mon–Fri 9am–5.30pm, Sat–Sun 10am–5.30pm; map p.132 C2 Hongqiao showroom: 1985 Hongqiao Road, near Hongxu Road; tel: 6219 7802; daily 9.30am–6pm

Lilli Makinson has created a tasteful collection of jewellery featuring semi-precious stones, as well as fashion

accessories and gift items. Silk photo albums, embroidered evening clutches and mah-jong tile bracelets are among the highlights.

Madame Mao's Dowry
207 Fumin Road, between Changle and Julu Roads; tel: 5403 3551; www.madamemaos dowry.com; daily 10am–7pm; Metro: Line 1, Changshu; Bus: 26; map p.136 C4

This store features an interesting collection of goods from the past that have come to symbolise Chinese sensibilities, such as enamelled thermoses with painted flowers, and classical Chinese clothing. It also has an extensive collection of photos and posters from the Cultural Revolution era.

Nanjing Pearl City
558 Nanjing East Road; daily 10am–10pm; Metro: Line 2, Nanjing East; map p.134 B3

Located on the second and third floors, this is a smaller version of the Hongqiao Pearl Market on Hongmei Road near Yan'an Road, with dozens of shops vigorously competing for busi-

of cafés with alfresco seating crowd the narrow lanes (Metro: Line 1, Shaanxi, then taxi).
SEE ALSO FASHION, P.56, 59

Uniquely Shanghai
Annabel Lee
Bund location: No.1, Lane 8, Zhongshan East Road; tel: 6445 8218; www.annabellee.com; daily 10am–10pm; Metro: Line 2, Nanjing East; map p.140 B1 Xintiandi location: North Square No. 3, 181 Taikang Road, near Huangpi South Road; tel: 6320 0045; daily 10am–10.30pm; map p.137 E2

A consortium of Asian designers have gathered an elegant collection of giftwares and home accessories, in high-quality silk, linen and

ness, but this one is more conveniently located. Pearls and other semi-precious stones in both finished and unfinished products are sold in abundance.

Platane

127 Yongfu Road, near Fuxing West Road; tel: 6433 6387; Mon–Sat 10am–7pm, Sun noon–7pm Also, 156 Taikang Road, near Sinan Road; tel: 6466 2495; Mon–Fri 10am–8pm, Sat–Sun 11am–8pm; map p.136 B3

Opened by a French national, this giftware and accessories shop oozes with class and has impeccable taste. Many of the items are imported, but some are locally sourced. The new location on Taikang Road proper (not within the alleyways) is larger than the Yongfu location and features a greater selection.

Shanghai Drama and Costume Shop

181 Henan Middle Road, near Jiujiang Road; tel: 6322 2604; Metro: Line 2, Nanjing East; map p.134 B3

This dusty old store features a huge collection of Chinese opera costumes. Although the staff don't speak English, it is an excellent place for browsing through the colourful costumes for stage or for fun. There is not much leeway for bargaining, unless you are buying in bulk.

Spin

758 Julu Road, near Fumin Road, Bldg 3, 1/F; tel: 6279 2545; daily 11am–9.30pm; Metro: Line 1, Shaanxi; map p.137 C4

Tucked inside the back of a parking lot, this gem of a shop specialises in handmade celadon porcelain. The selection varies from the tra-

ditional to the avant-garde styles of teapots, vases, cups, plates and decanters. Many are limited editions, which makes for an affordable piece of exclusivity.

Suzhou Cobblers

Room 101, 17 Fuzhou Road, near Zhongshan Road; tel: 6321 7087; daily 10am–6pm; Metro: Line 2, Nanjing East; map p.140 B2

Denise Huang has designed a sweet collection of colourful hand-embroidered slippers, soft shoes and baby clothes, featuring traditional Chinese motifs such as bamboo, goldfish and cherry blossoms. Located off the Bund, it's a charming little store filled with collectables.

Left and above left: Nanjing Road East.
Above and right: Spin.

119

Sports

Although Shanghai has produced world-class athletes like basketball player Yao Ming and Olympic gold medal hurdler Liu Xiang, its citizens are generally more interested in money than in sports, and as a result, the city's sporting culture is not very robust. Interest in seasonal spectator sports like basketball and football is growing, however, and enthusiasm for golf is also on the rise. Annual events like the Shanghai ATP Masters tennis tournament and the Formula One Grand Prix also generate significant passion, because they attract famous stars, and because they take place in brand-new, state-of-the-art facilities.

Golf

Golf is becoming more popular in Shanghai, although it remains a game for the wealthy, as the best courses are for members only, and the others are expensive. On a weekday, you could expect to pay Rmb600 to 900, and at the weekend, more than Rmb1,500, which includes a caddy. Golfers who are accustomed to courses with beautifully manicured natural landscapes will need to adjust their expectations. The Shanghai-area golf courses were originally flat farmland, so trees must be planted and babbling brooks manufactured. The two best courses in Shanghai are Sheshan Golf Club and Tomson Golf Course, but they are restricted to members only.

Binhai Golf

Binhai Resort, Nanhui; reservation tel: 3800 1888; information tel: 5805 8888; www.binhaigolf.com/home.html; Rmb 760 weekdays, 1,560 weekends, club rental Rmb200, shoes Rmb50

For tourists, the best option might be Binhai golf course, about an hour from town, near the Pudong airport. It is relatively inexpensive and open to the public, and it offers a free shuttle bus from downtown Shanghai. Binhai has two 18-hole courses, and one of them, the Peter Thomson-designed Lake Course, is a long, 7,105-yard, par-73 course that includes a 629-yard par-five hole.

Yintao Golf

2222 Huqingping Highway, Qingpu District; tel: 6976 2222; Rmb690 weekdays, 990 weekends

Left: Western sports such as basketball and Formula One (**below left**) have become very popular. **Below:** yoga still plays a large part in Chinese life.

venue in the world. The track was built on 40,000 concrete pylons in the Anting suburb in western Shanghai, with a layout that guarantees excitement: shaped like the Chinese character shang, used in the word Shanghai, the course includes hairpin turns and long straight sections that provide plenty of opportunity for racers to overtake one another. In 2009, the Formula One Grand Prix race was moved from October to April, but nobody knows whether that will be its permanent slot. Check www.formula1.com for updated information.

Qizhong Stadium
5500, Yuan Jiang Road, Minhang District, about an hour from downtown
This new US$290 million, Japanese-designed arena, home to the Shanghai ATP Masters tennis tournament that is held every October, is a beauty. The roof has eight interlocking, sliding steel plates that open and close like a lotus flower, according to the weather, and it can hold 15,000 spectators for tennis, basketball and pop music concerts.

Another good option for visitors is Yintao, which is just 20km (12 miles) from downtown Shanghai. It has a single 18-hole course, also designed by five-time British Open winner Peter Thomson, and it is open to non-members.

Spectator Sports
BASKETBALL
The Shanghai Sharks play in the Chinese Basketball Association league, and current NBA star Yao Ming, who once played for the Sharks, is now the team's owner. The league has been in existence since 1994, and although it continues to struggle, it has developed a small but loyal following. The Sharks play in little **Luwan Stadium** in the old French Concession South, from November to April.

Luwan Stadium
128 Zhaojiabang Road, tel: 6427 8673; Metro: Line 4, Damuqiao, then short taxi ride; map p.137 C1

FOOTBALL
The Shanghai Shenhua play in the Chinese Football Association Super League, or CSL, the top league in China. The season begins in March and ends in November, with games about once a week, usually on Saturdays.

Hongkou Stadium
444 Jiangwan Road East; tickets and information tel: 5666 8969; www.shenhuafc.com.cn (Chinese only); Metro: Lines 3, 8, Hongkou Football Stadium; Bus: 18, 939

Venues
Formula One Racetrack
Shanghai's 5.5km (3½-mile), US$320 million Formula One racetrack is the most expensive and sophisticated F1

Transport

Traffic in Shanghai can seem hazardous, but there is a certain amount of order in the chaos, as local residents have little trouble navigating the roads that are crowded with bikes, tricycles, scooters and an increasing number of cars. The easiest way to get around in Shanghai is by taxi or Metro, but few taxi drivers speak English, so it is best to have the *pinyin* (romanisation of the Chinese word) or the Chinese characters of your destination written out, with a cross street as reference. The Metro is to be avoided during rush hour, when etiquette disappears and pushing and shoving prevail.

Arriving by Air

Pudong International Airport (www.shanghaiairport.com) is Shanghai's main international airport, and is located 30km (19 miles) east of the city centre. It is one of the country's busiest airports, and is set to be busier with work under way on a third terminal and two new runways. **Hongqiao Airport** is the primary domestic airport, and is at the western end of the city. It serves only two international flights, one from Japan and the other from Korea. The Maglev train line is expected to connect the two airports by 2010, cutting travel time from about 90 minutes to just 15.

Arriving by Sea

Set to become a major cruise-liner destination, Shanghai has built the **Shanghai Port International Cruise Terminal** and another terminal on **Potai Bay** in Wusong Port to handle the larger vessels that are unable to pass under the Yangpu Bridge. A third terminal is located at the mouth of the **Yangtze**.

Train travel in China is for the masses, and it gives visitors a view not only of the passing landscape outside the window, but also an intimate view of local life and a chance, if you speak some Mandarin or find an English-speaker, to meet Chinese fellow travellers.

Arriving by Train

Train services have improved dramatically in recent years, cutting travel time by hours to nearby locations such as Suzhou, Hangzhou and Nanjing. Work is proceeding rapidly on the high-speed Beijing–Shanghai route, due to be completed sometime after 2010. Arrival in Shanghai from the north is usually at the Shanghai Railway Station, while the beautiful new Shanghai South Railway Station serves trains that connect to southern China. Both offer access to Metro lines and feature fast-moving taxi queues.

Arriving by Coach/Bus

The three main bus terminals are located south of People's Park, next to Shanghai Stadium and next to Hongkou

Above: stepping aboard the Maglev train. **Right:** Shanghai by car.

Left: traffic forming an orderly queue behind the warden.

company will help you locate it. Drivers for the most part are honest, though there have been cases of overcharging foreign visitors.

Ten **airport bus shuttle** lines serve the airport, leaving at 15- to 25-minute intervals. Follow the signs for the bus shuttle across a walkway towards the parking lot. The most useful lines are Line 1, which goes to the domestic airport, and Line 2, which goes to Jing'an Temple in the city centre, where you can catch a taxi to your final destination.

Line 3 goes to Galaxy Hotel in western Shanghai via Xujiahui, while Line 5 goes to the Shanghai Railway Station. A fare collector will come on board and give change if necessary. The prices, depending on destination, range from Rmb18 to 30. Though buses tend to be old, they are adequate, and are heated in winter and air-conditioned in summer.

The **Maglev** (short for magnetic levitation) train takes passengers from the airport to Longyang Station, which connects to Metro Line

Stadium. Routes connect Shanghai to nearby destinations such as Sheshan resort, Jinshan beach and Nanhui's Wild Animal Park, as well as more distant locations such as Suzhou, Hangzhou and Ningbo. These terminals are located near Metro lines, and are also served by taxi queues (tel: 6426 5555).

Getting Around

FROM PUDONG INTER-
NATIONAL AIRPORT
The **taxi** queue can be found

outside the arrival hall to the left as you exit. Flagfall is Rmb12 for the first three kilometres and Rmb2.4 for every additional kilometre, with flagfall increasing to Rmb16 after 11pm.

A ride from the airport to People's Square should cost less than Rmb200. All taxis are required to produce a receipt, and it's a good idea to keep it in case there is a dispute over the fare, or if you leave something behind. If you do leave something behind, the taxi

Taxi companies also have metered vans that are handy for those travelling with a large group or with lots of luggage. They are called *mianbao chi*, or bread cars, because of their bread-loaf shape, and can be found at the airport or ordered through a taxi company.

2. Billed as one of the fastest trains in the world, it can reach 430kmph (270mph), but lately, to save electricity, it has been travelling at 'just' 300kmph (190mph). Service begins from 6.45am to 9.30pm and costs Rmb50 for a one-way trip; if you show your boarding pass, the ticket is Rmb40. Longyang Station is in a distant suburb, with nothing useful anywhere in the area, but plans are under way to connect the Maglev to the domestic airport in Hongqiao.

CITY TRANSPORT
Taxi
About 40,000 taxicabs ply the roads in Shanghai, mak-

ing them a convenient way to get around. During rush hour or when it is raining, taxis are very scarce indeed, but at other times they are quite plentiful. The three main taxi companies are **Dazhong** (tel: 6258 1688), **Bashi** (tel: 6431 2788) and **Jinjiang** (tel: 6275 8800). All drivers have a photo and registered taxi number on a placard, and in an effort to offer incentives to those who know their city streets, a star system has been devised as indicated on their ID placards: five stars for those with excellent knowledge and service skills, to one star for those who have neither.

Metro
Shanghai has a total of 11 Metro lines planned, with nine currently in operation. Line 2 is the main east–west connector, Line 4 does a circle around the ring road and loops into Pudong, while the very useful Line 1 cuts a diagonal line through the city centre heading north and south. As with buses, a walk of several blocks may be necessary. For some destinations, it may be better to take the Metro to the closest stop, then a taxi.

Buses
The city bus network is extensive and inexpensive at Rmb2 per zone (children under 1.2m/3ft 11ins ride for free) collected upon boarding. The only deficit for visitors is that

moderate Chinese skills are necessary and the buses get crowded during rush hour. Buses are numbered and their routes are indicated in Chinese and Pinyin at all bus stops, with intersections or major landmarks such as parks serving as a reference point. Some popular routes include bus 911 that goes from the Shanghai Zoo to Laoximen (several blocks from Yuyuan Garden), bus 20 from Zhongshan Park to the Bund, and bus 104 from Longhua Temple area to the Shanghai Railway Station. The website http://msittig.wubi.org/bus lists all routes in English.

Tours

Bus Tours

A double-decker, open-air bus goes from Shanghai Stadium in Xujiahui to the Bund area for Rmb3. It offers a pleasant ride through the leafy streets of the French Concession along Hengshan Road and the retail hub of

Left and above: two-wheeled transport is as popular as elsewhere in Asia.

Huaihai Road towards the Old Town to the east of the city. Then it loops around Renmin Road on the return trip. It's best to board along Hengshan or Huaihai Roads going eastbound to avoid the traffic-filled streets of Xujiahui, and alight near the Bund or Yuyuan Garden.

Bike Tour

To get a feel for the real Shanghai, tour the city on the seat of a bike instead of a coach. Two companies offers day and night guided trips of the city, which can take you across Puxi through the Old Town and on a ferry to Pudong and back again. Tours takes about three to four hours depending on the length of stops. Fees range

> Stored-value transit cards can be purchased in Metro stations for an Rmb20 deposit and can be used in taxis, buses and Metro trains. Metro stations also have vending machines where you can add value to the cards, and the machines offer an English instruction option.

> Honking your horn is actually illegal on the streets of Shanghai, not that you would know it. People generally don't take offence and ignore horns anyway, and the result is a non-stop blare of deafening horns.

from Rmb150–180 and include bike rental, helmet and ferry fare, or Rmb80 for bicycle rental alone (Cycle China; www.cyclechina.com; bato@cyclechina.com; mobile tel: 86 1391 707 1775; China Cycle Tours; www.chinacycletours.com; tel: 1376 111 5050).

Something Different

Shanghai Sideways offers guided tours in sidecars driven by foreign guides, many of whom are long-term residents of the city. Options range from shopping tours to night tours, and from old Shanghai sights to new Shanghai sights. Fees include helmets and raingear if necessary, and range from Rmb600 to Rmb1,000 per passenger, depending on group size (www.shanghaisideways.com; tel: 150 2111 2451).

Walks and Views

Seen from above, Shanghai is a vast sea of tiled rooftops, skyscrapers and elevated highways, and the city has many high towers that present these fine views. From high in the air, Shanghai is a surprising contrast of old next to new, of crowded markets and narrow lane-house neighbourhoods adjacent to modern superstructures and shopping centres and five-star hotels. But as impressive as these views are, many of the city's charms are best seen at street level, and here too, the visitor is in luck, because Shanghai is filled with unique and enjoyable walks.

Best Views

Jinmao Tower

88 Century Boulevard, Pudong; tel: 5047 5101; www.jinmao88.com; daily 8am–9pm; admission; Metro: Line 2, Lujiazui; map p.135 E3

The number eight, a lucky number for the Chinese, plays a strong role in this lovely tower with the pagoda-styled top. It has 88 storeys, and eight exterior steel columns and eight exterior composite supercolumns that hold up the octagonal structure, and its horizontal sections get progressively smaller by one eighth, lending it a superb symmetry unequalled by any other building in Shanghai. The observation deck on the 88th floor offers panoramic vistas of the city and a close-up view of the Shanghai World Financial Centre next door. The **Grand Hyatt** lobby on the 53rd floor also offers fine views.
SEE ALSO ARCHITECTURE, P.33; HOTELS, P.77

New Heights

7/F, Three on the Bund, 3 Zhongshan East No. 1 Road, by Guangdong Road; tel: 6321 0909; www.threeonthebund.com; daily, restaurant 11am–2.30pm, 5.30–10.30pm, bar 11.30–1am; Metro: Line 2, Nanjing East; map p.140 B1

Though not as prestigious as neighbouring Jean Georges and M on the Bund, New Heights has the best patio rooftops view of any building on the Bund. It is an ideal location for pre-dinner drinks, and a perfect place for photos of the Pudong skyline.
SEE ALSO RESTAURANTS, P.101

Oriental Pearl Tower

1 Century Boulevard, Pudong; tel: 5879 1888; daily 8.30am–

Take the elevator up to the deck of the **Nanpu Bridge** – it's the one with the corkscrew spiral on ramp – for a high-octane walk and eagle-eye views of both sides of the city, and of the ceaselessly throbbing river itself. Located on the Puxi side by the bus terminal at Lujiabang and Zhongshan South roads, the elevator ride is Rmb10, a genuine bargain, and one that few people know about. Metro: Line 8, Lujiabang, then taxi; Bus: 43, 81, 92, 801, 802, 869, 910, 931.

Above: Bund Promenade.
Right: ascending Lupu Bridge.

Left: Bund at night.

10pm; admission; Metro: Line 2, Lujiazui; map p.135 E3

When completed in 2008, this 492m (1,614ft) tower – often called the bottle opener – was the second-tallest building in the world at the time of publishing, after Taipei 101. One of the three levels of observation deck features a glass-bottomed walkway across the trapezoidal hole at the tip of the building, giving visitors a thrilling walk. Aerial views can also be had from the **Park Hyatt** hotel, located from the 79th floor up. On gusty and cloudy evenings, you can watch the Jinmao Tower and the rest of the city appear and disappear behind dramatic, fast-moving mists.

SEE ALSO ARCHITECTURE, P.33; HOTELS, P.77

Vue Bar

Hyatt on the Bund; 32–33/F, 199 Huangpu Road, by Wuchang Road; tel: 6393 1234 ext 6348; www. shanghai.bund.hyatt.com, 6pm–late; Metro: Line 2, Nanjing East, then taxi; Bus: 33, 37; map p.135 C4

9.30pm; admission; Metro: Line 2, Lujiazui; map p.135 D4

This 468m (1,535ft) tower, with its red 'pearls' and rocket-like base, was the tallest structure in Shanghai when it was completed in 1994. Now it is dwarfed by the 'big three' towers of Pudong: the Jinmao, the Shanghai World Financial Centre and the soon-to-be-completed Shanghai Tower.

The Pearl Tower is the best of the observation decks from a viewing perspective, because of its waterfront location and unobstructed 360-degree views.

SEE ALSO ARCHITECTURE, P.32, 33

Shanghai World Financial Centre

100 Century Boulevard, Pudong; tel: 3867 2008/400 1100 555; daily 8am–11pm, last entry

The view from the Hyatt's rooftop bar is guaranteed to impress: it is the best outdoor view in Shanghai, bar none, with a dramatic perspective of the Bund to the south and the vertical towers of Pudong to the east, along with the never-ending surge of boat traffic on the Huangpu River. The night scene, with the twinkling neon signs, makes the great view even more spectacular, and another highlight is the newly refurbished Waibaidu Bridge, originally built in 1907, with its coloured fluorescent lights glowing nearby. SEE ALSO BARS AND CAFÉS, P.37; HOTELS, P.71

River Cruises

Boat rides on the Huangpu River are a fine way to see the nitty-gritty of the Chinese economic miracle, as well as the bright lights of Pudong and the old buildings of the Bund. Most excursions cost Rmb45–60 during the day, and a little more at night, and they sail north to the Yangpu Bridge, then south to the Nanpu Bridge, a route that encompasses most of downtown Shanghai, including the Expo site, the Bund and downtown Pudong. Longer cruises sail north up the Huangpu and into the Yangtze River itself, a three-hour, 60km (37-mile) journey that costs Rmb90–120. At press time, the Bund ferry dock was under renovation, so telephone numbers and websites were unavailable.

A variety of **guided tours** are available. Spencer Dodington, an architect from the United States, shares his love and knowledge of Shanghai's historic buildings (http://luxury conciergechina.com; tel: 135 0166 2908). Anne Warr is an Australian architect who has published a book detailing 270 of Shanghai's best buildings (www.walkshanghai.com), and who also gives excellent, knowledgeable tours. Photographer Wang Gang Feng, a native of Shanghai, opens doors to people's homes on his tours and provides a perspective rarely seen by outsiders (www.gangofone.com.cn; tel: 139 0160 8284).

Walks

Bund Pedestrian Walkway and ferry to Pudong Promenade

Start at the Monument to the People's Heroes, the concrete obelisk at the north of the Bund, where there is a small exhibition of old photos. Then start south along the Bund walkway, which recently reopened after a long renovation. It gives visitors a great perspective on the classical buildings of the Bund, the symbolic icons of old Shanghai. Walk south and see the famous Fairmont Peace Hotel with its triangular green rooftop, the Customs House with its clock tower ringing out 'The East is Red' every quarter-hour, and the grand old Hongkong and Shanghai Bank Building that is now the Pudong Development Bank. Then go down to street level at the south end of the Bund, and take the local Dongjin ferry across the river to the Pudong side, and walk north until you reach the Pudong Promenade park, which features fine views of the Bund as well as a selection of cafés and restaurants.

Then comes a real treat: return to the Bund in the **Bund Sightseeing Tunnel**, a 650m (2,133ft) toy train ride under the Huangpu River that is filled with flashing psychedelic lights and a nonsensical soundtrack. This ride never fails to impress – trust us (located near the base of the Oriental Pearl Tower; tel: 5888 6000; Mon–Thur 8am–10.30pm, Fri–Sun 8am–11pm; admission; Metro: Line 1, Lujiazui, or on the Bund side, Nanjing East).

Duolun Road

In the northern district of Hongkou is Duolun Road, a street that in the 1930s was home to a number of notable literary figures such as **Lu Xun**, Mao Dun and the poet Guo Moruo. Start the walk at the north junction of Sichuan North Road and Duolun Road, where the brass placards explain the street's back-story. The mile-long

cobblestone street is for pedestrians only, though scooters and bikes keep the pace lively. The road is lined with distinctive period architecture and small stores selling antique-looking knick-knacks. Takes an hour or so.

SEE ALSO FILM AND LITERATURE, P.60

Fuxing West Road

This is one of Shanghai's most charming neighbourhoods, in the nicest part of the former French Concession. The area is filled with lane-houses, 1930s Art Deco apartment buildings and full-on details of daily Shanghai life. Get started on Fuxing West Road and Urumqi Road, a corner that features the Iranian Embassy. Walk west and turn left on Yongfu Road, where you'll find Platane, a small gift shop (at No. 127; Mon–Sat 10am–7pm, Sun noon–7pm; tel: 6433 6387) and gaze at the grounds of **Yongfoo Elite**, a clubhouse that once

served as consulates for the UK, Russia and Vietnam (200 Yongfu Road, near Hunan Road; tel: 5466 2727), and is now a restaurant of fading quality. Take a right at Hunan Road and again at Wukang Road, where you'll find the polished retail complex of Ferguson Lane (376 Wukang Road), which features boutiques, a French bistro, florist, spa and art gallery. Continue north and turn left on Fuxing West Road, and go past Gaoyou Road until you get to Le Passage (299 Fuxing West Road), a 1932 retail complex that has been refurbished and now houses boutiques, galleries and Ginger Café in the back. To finish the walk, continue along Fuxing until you get to Huashan Road, then take a right and continue along until you see the entrance to the Dingshan Gardens, and enjoy a walk in the park (Metro: Line 1, Changshu, walk west along Huaihai Road to Fuxing Middle Road. Takes two to three hours).

Above: Taikang Lu **Left:** Bund walkway.

Atlas

The following streetplan of Shanghai makes it easy to find the attractions listed in our A–Z section. A selective index to streets and sights will help you find other locations throughout the city.

Map Legend

Expressway		Railway	
Divided highway		Ferry	
Main road		Bus station	
Airport		Airport	
Minor road		Tourist information	
Footpath		Sight of interest	
Tunnel		Chinese temple	
Pedestrian area		Buddhist temple	
Notable building		Cathedral/church	
Park		Mosque	
Shopping mall/ market		Synagogue	
Hotel		Museum/gallery	
Urban area		Theatre/concert hall	
Non urban area		Statue/monument	
		Post office	
		Library	
		Hospital	

p132	p133	p140	
		p134	p135
p136	p137	p138	p139

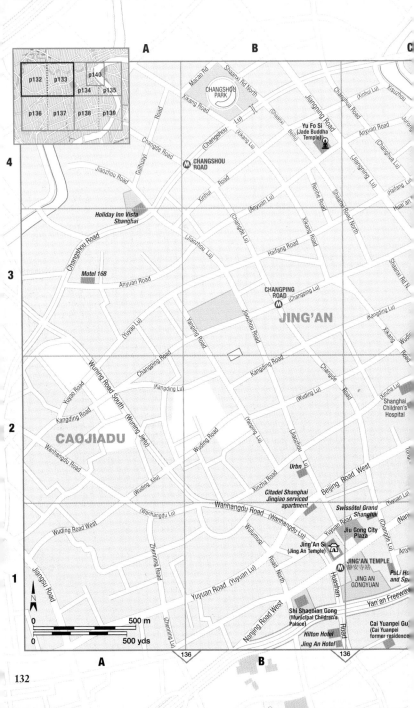

A B C

p132 | p133 | p140
p134 | p135
p136 | p137 | p138 | p139

4

Macao Rd

Shaanxi Rd North

CHANGSHOU PARK

Xikang Road

Jiangning Road

Changhua Road

(Xinhui Lu)

Xisuzhou

Anyuan Road

Jurong

Road

Changde Road

(Changshou Lu)

Xikang Road

(Shaanxi Bei)

Yu Fo Si
(Jade Buddha
Temple)

(Jiangning Lu)

(Changhua Lu)

Jiaozhou Road

Guihuayi

M CHANGSHOU
ROAD

Road

Xinhui

(Anyuan Lu)

Renhe Road

Shaanxi Road North

(Haifang Lu)

Huai'an

Holiday Inn Vista
Shanghai

(Jiaozhou Lu)

(Changde Lu)

Haifang Road

Xikang Road

Changshou Road

3

Motel 168

Anyuan Road

(Yuyao Lu)

Yanping Road

Jiaozhou Road

CHANGPING
ROAD
M (Changping Lu)

Shaanxi Rd N

(Kangding Lu)

JING'AN

Xikang

Wudin

Changping Road

(Kangding Lu)

Kangding Road

Changde

Road

(Xinzha Lu)

Shanghai
Children's
Hospital

2

CAOJIADU

Yuyao Road

Wuning Road South

Kangding Road

(Wuning Jielu)

Wuding Road

(Wuding Lu)

(Jiaozhou Lu)

Urbn
Lu

Beijing Road West

Tuji

Wanhangdu Road

(Yuyao Lu)

(Wanhangdu Lu)

Xinzha Road

Citadel Shanghai
Jinqiao serviced
apartment

Wanhangdu Road (Wanhangdu Lu)

Yuyuan

Swissôtel Grand
Shanghai

(Nan

(Changde Lu)

Yuyuan Lu

1

Jiangsu Road

(Wanhangdu Lu)

Wuding Road West

Zhenning Road

(Wulumuqi)

Wuding
Road North

Yuyuan Road (Yuyuan Lu)

Nanjing Road West

(Zhenning Lu)

Jiu Gong City
Plaza

Jing'An Si
(Jing An Temple)

JING'AN TEMPLE
静安寺站
M

JING AN
GONGYUAN

PuLi Ho
and Sp

Huashan

Road

Yan'an Freeway

Shi Shaonian Gong
(Municipal Children's
Palace)

Hilton Hotel

Jing An Hotel

Cai Yuanpei Gu
(Cai Yuanpei
former residence

Anyi

N

0   500 m
0   500 yds

A | 136 | B | 136

132

Tibet (Xizang) Rd N
Gonghe Road (Gonghe Lu)
Chang'an Road
Guangfu Road
Chang'an Road
Yutong Rd
Puji Road
Hengfeng Road (Hengfeng Lu)
Minli Road
Meiyuan
(Hanzhong Lu)
Huashing Rd
Huashang Rd
Datong Road
Nanjing Road
Xinjiang Road
Wuchten Road
Menggu Road
Jinyuan
Qufu Road
Guoqing Road

Hengfeng Road Bus Interchange
HANZHONG ROAD 漢中路站
Hengtong Road
Chang'an
Hanzhong Rd
Guangfu Rd
QUFU ROAD 曲阜路站

(Huai an Lu)
Suzhou Creek (Wusong)
Shichou Creek (Xuzhou Lu)
Hengfeng Rd
Guangfu Rd
Chang'an
Suzhouhe Road
(Kangding Lu)
Shimen No.2 Road (Shimen 2-Lu)
Datian Road
(Xinzha Lu)
(Guangfu Lu)
(Suzhouha Lu)

North-South Freeway (elevated)

XINZHA ROAD 新閘路站
Xinzha Road
Wenzhou Rd
Huanghe Rd
Xinchang Road
Xinjiang Road

Kangding Road
Changhua Road
Xinzha Road
Jiangning Road
(Wuding Lu)
Taixing Road
Zhangshuhe Road
(Datian Lu)
Shanghaiguan Road
Cixi Road
(Beijing Xilu)
Beijing Road East
Guling Road

3

NI CHENG QIAO

Park Hotel

(Shaanxi Beilu)
Jiangning Road
(Jiangning Lu)
Xinzha Road
Changhua Road
(Taixing Lu)
Zhangshuhe Road
Fengyang Road
Road
(Fengyang Lu)
Xinchang Road
PEOPLE'S SQUARE 人民廣場站
Daguangming Dian Ying (Grand Cinema)

Beijing Road West
Beijing Road West
(Nanjing Xilu)
Nanjing Road West

Youtai Jiaotang (Ohel Rachel Synagogue)
(Beijing Xilu)
WEST NANJING ROAD 南京西路站
JW Marriott Hotel

Majestic Theatre
JIA Shanghai
Ruitai Jimgan Hôtel
Haifang Road
Nanyang Rd
Maoming Road
Taixing Road
Wujiang
Qinghai Road
Jiangyin Road
Chongqing
Central Plaza

Westgate Mall
CITIC Square
Nanjing Road West
(Nanhai Lu)
Shimen No.1 Road (Shimen 1-Lu)
Weihai Road
Wusheng Rd (Wusheng Lu)
Huangpi Road North
Nanjing Road West
Jiangyin Road

2

Shanghai Centre serviced apartment
rtman z-Carlton
Plaza 66
Shaanxi Rd N
(Nanhai Lu)
(Weihai Lu)
Weihai Road (Weihai Lu)
Weihai Road
(Dagu)

Shanghai angcheng (anghai Centre))
JC Mandarin
Four Seasons Shanghai
Maoming Beilu
Dagu Road
Yan'an Chengdu Interchange

Shanghai Zhanlan Zhongxin (Shanghai Exhibition Centre)

Central Yan'an Road (Yan'an Zhonglu)
Central Yan'an Road (Yan'an Zhonglu)
(elevated)
Hengshan Male Bieshu (Hengshan Moller Villa)
Julu Road

1

Julu Lu
Shaanxi Rd N
Maoming
Ruijin No.2 Road (Ruijin 2-Lu)
Lanxin Daxiyuan (Lyceum Theatre)
Jinjang Tower
Changle
Chengdu Rd S
Central Huaihai Road
Chongqing Road South (Chongqing Beilu)

Motel 268
Jinxian (Lu)
Okura Garden Hotel
Jinjan Hotel
Changle Road
Jinxian Road
Changle (Lu)
Maoming South
Isetan
Xing'an Rd

Changle Road South

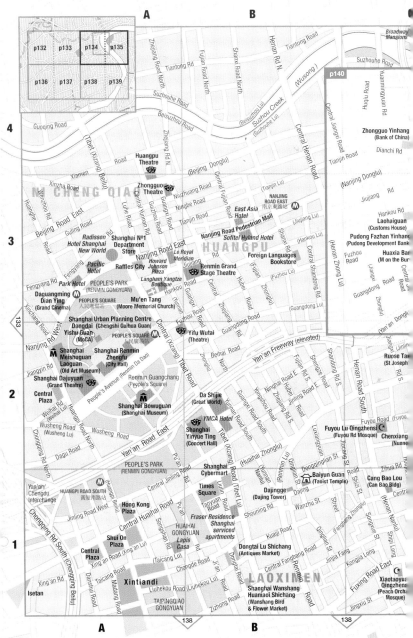

A   **B**   **C**

| p132 | p133 | p134 | p135 |
| p136 | p137 | p138 | p139 |

Broadway Mansions

Suzhouhe Road

p140

4

Guoqing Road

Suzhouhe Road

Beisuzhou Road

Zhongguo Yinhang
(Bank of China)

Tianjin Road

Dianchi Rd

Huangpu
Theatre

Xinzha Road

WU CHENG QIAO

Beijing Road East

Zhongguo
Theatre

Guling Road

(Nanjing Donglu)

3

Radisson
Hotel Shanghai
New World

Shanghai No1
Department
Store

East Asia
Hotel

NANJING
ROAD EAST
南京東路站

Jiujiang

Hankou Rd

Laohaiguan
(Customs House)

Nanjing Road East

Nanjing Road Pedestrian Mall

Le Royal
Meridien

Sofitel Hyland Hotel

Pudong Fazhan Yinhang
(Pudong Development Bank)

Pacific
Hotel

Howard
Johnson
Plaza

Raffles City

Foreign Languages
Bookstore

Huaxia Bar
(M on the Bund)

Fengyang Rd

Park Hotel
PEOPLE'S PARK
(RENMIN GONGYUAN)

Langham Yangtze
Boutique

Renmin Grand
Stage Theatre

Fuzhou

Guangdong Road

Daguangming
Dian Ying
(Grand Cinema)

PEOPLE'S SQUARE
人民廣場站

Mu'en Tang
(Moore Memorial Church)

Guangdong Road

133

Nanjing Rd West

Shanghai Urban Planning Centre
Danggdai (Chengshi Guihua Guan)
Yishu Guan
(MoCA)

PEOPLE'S SQUARE
人民廣場站

Yifu Wutai
(Theatre)

Ruose Tai
(St Joseph

Jiangyin Rd

Shanghai
Meishuguan
Laoguan
(Old Art Museum)

Shanghai Renmin
Zhengfu
(City Hall)

Beihai Road

Shanghai Dajuyuan
(Grand Theatre)

Renmin Guangchang
(People's Square)

2

Central
Plaza

People's Avenue (Renmin Da Dao)

Shanghai Bowuguan
(Shanghai Museum)

Da Shijie
(Great World)

Weihai Rd
(Weihai Lu)

Yan'an Road East

YMCA Hotel

Fuyou Lu Qingzhensi
(Fuyou Rd Mosque)

Chenxiang
(Nunne

Wusheng Road
(Wusheng Lu)

Wusheng Road

Shanghai
Yinyue Ting
(Concert Hall)

Dagu Road

Baiyun Guan
(Taoist Temple)

Cang Bao Lou
(Can Bao Bldg)

PEOPLE'S PARK
(RENMIN GONGYUAN)

Shanghai
Cybermart

Dajingge
(Dajing Tower)

Yan'an/
Chengdu
Interchange

HUAIHAI ROAD SOUTH
黃陂南路站

Times
Square

Hong Kong
Plaza

Fraser Residence
Shanghai
serviced
apartments

Dongtai Lu Shichang
(Antiques Market)

Zihua Rd

Xiaotaoyua
Qingzhens
(Peach Orcha
Mosque)

1

Central
Plaza

Shui On
Plaza

HUAIHAI
GONGYUAN

Lapis
Casa

LAOXIMEN

Isetan

Xing'an Rd

Xintiandi

TAI(PINGQIAO)
GONGYUAN

Shanghai Wanshang
Huaniaoi Shichang
(Wanshang Bird
& Flower Market)

Fuxing Road East

Jingxiu St

A   **138**   **B**   **138**

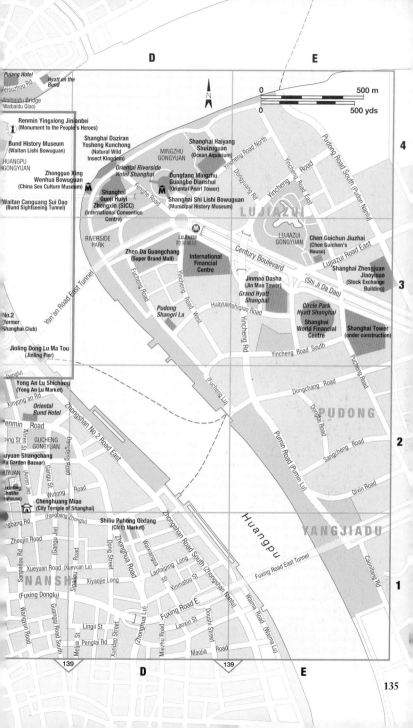

D   E

Pujang Hotel

Hyatt on the Bund

Weisuzhou Rd

Waibaidu Bridge
(Waibaidu Qiao)

Renmin Yingxiong Jinianbei
(Monument to the People's Heroes)

Bund History Museum
(Waitan Lishi Bowuguan)

HUANGPU
GONGYUAN

**Zhongguo Xing
Wenhua Bowuguan**
(China Sex Culture Museum)

Waitan Canguang Sui Dao
(Bund Sightseeing Tunnel)

**Shanghai Daziran
Yesheng Kunchong**
(Natural Wild
Insect Kingdom)

MINGZHU
GONGYUAN

**Shanghai Haiyang
Shuizuguan**
(Ocean Aquarium)

*Oriental Riverside
Hotel Shanghai*

**Dongfang Mingzhu
Guangbo Dianshui**
(Oriental Pearl Tower)

**Shanghai
Guoji Huiyi
Zhongxin (SICC)**
(International
Convention
Centre)

Fenghe Road

Shanghai Shi Lishi Bowuguan
(Municipal History Museum)

LUJIAZUI

Yincheng Road North

Dongyuang Rd

Yincheng Road East

Yincheng
Road

Pudong Road South (Pudon Nanlu)

4

RIVERSIDE
PARK

Zhen Da Guangchang
(Super Brand Mall)

LUJIAZUI
陆家嘴站

LUJIAZUI
GONGYUAN

Chen Guichun Jiuzhai
(Chen Guichen's
House)

Fucheng
Road

Yincheng
Road West

**International
Financial
Centre**

Century Boulevard

Lujiazui Road East

**Shanghai Zhengjuan
Jiaoyisuo**
(Stock Exchange
Building)

3

No.2
(former
Shanghai Club)

Yan'an Road East Tunnel

*Pudong
Shangri La*

Huayuanshiqiao Road

Jinmao Dasha
(Jin Mao Tower)

*Grand Hyatt
Shanghai*

(Shi Ji Da Dao)

**Circle Park
Hyatt Shanghai**

**Shanghai
World Financial
Centre**

Shanghai Tower
(under construction)

Jinling Dong Lu Ma Tou
(Jinling Pier)

Donglu

Yincheng Rd

Yincheng Road South

Dongchang Road

(Fucheng Lu)

PUDONG

Yong An Lu Shichang
(Yong An Lu Market)

*Oriental
Bund Hotel*

Xinyong'an Rd

enmin   Road

Zhongshan No.2 Road East

Pangfeng Road

Pumin Road (Pumin Lu)

Dongli Road

Sangcheng Road

2

bing St

**GUCHENG
GONGYUAN**

Anren St

Gangu St

Road

Qixin Road

uyuan Shangchang
Yu Garden Bazaar)

UYUAN

uxinting
hashe
eahouse)

Anren Jiel

Wutong

Chenghuang Miao
(City Temple of Shanghai)

(Fangbang Zhonglu)

Shiliu Puhong Qixtang
(Cloth Market)

Zhongshan Road South (Zhongtan Nanlu)

Waikangwa

Huangpu

YANGJIADU

ngbang Rd

Zhoujin Road

(Gangu) Road

Zhongchua Road

Dong Street

Laotaiping Long

Xinmatou St

1

Sanqiao Rd

Xueyuan Road (Xueyuan Lu)

Sipailou Rd

Xiyaojie Long

Fuxing Road East Tunnel

Waima Road (Waima Lu)

Caonilang Rd

NANSHI

(Fuxing Donglu)

Guangqi Road South

Wangwun Road

Meilia St

Lingii St

Penglai Rd

Xundao Street

(Zhonghua Lu)

Miezhu Road

Fuxing Road E.

Laoxin St

Doushi Street

Maojia   Road

Wangwun Road

D   139   139   E

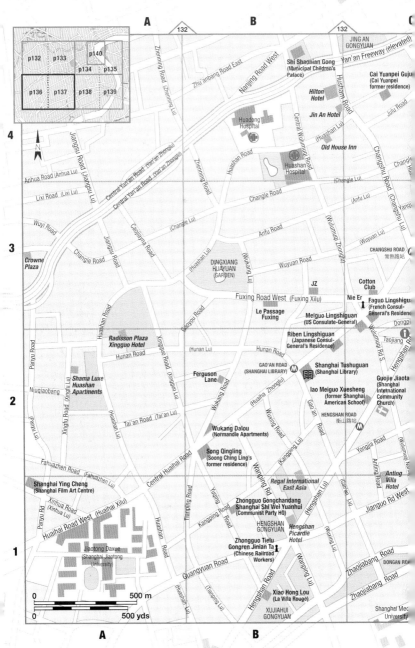

A · 132 · B · 132 · C

p132 | p133 | p140
p134 | p135
p136 | p137 | p138 | p139

4

Zhenning Road East (Zhenning Lu)

Zhu'anbang Road East

Nanjing Road West

Shi Shaonian Gong
(Municipal Children's Palace)

JING AN GONGYUAN

Yan'an Freeway (elevated)

Cai Yuanpei Guju
(Cai Yuanpei former residence)

Julu Road

Hilton Hotel

Jin An Hotel

Old House Inn

Huadong Hospital

Central Wulumuqi Road (Huashan Lu)

Changshu Road (Changshu Lu)

Changle

Hu

Huashan Road

Huashan Hospital

Anhua Road (Anhua Lu)

Central Yan'an Road (Yan'an Zhonglu)

Lixi Road (Lixi Lu)

Zhenning Road

Changle Road

(Changle Lu)

(Anfu Lu)

Yang

3

Wuyi Road

Jiangsu Road (Jiangsu Lu)

Changle Road

Caojiayan Road

(Changle Lu)

(Huashan Lu)

Anfu Road

(Wulumuqi Zhonglu)

(Wuyuan Lu)

CHANGSHU ROAD
常熟路站

Crowne Plaza

DINGXIANG HUAYUAN
(GARDEN)

(Nujiang Lu)

Wuyuan Road

JZ

Nie Er

Cotton Club

Faguo Lingshiguan
(French Consul-General's Residence)

Fuxing Road West (Fuxing Xilu)

Le Passage Fuxing

Meiguo Lingshiguan
(US Consulate-General)

Dongpi

Gaoyou Road

Riben Lingshiguan
(Japanese Consul-General's Residence)

Wulumuqi Rd S.

Taojiang

Hengshan Road

2

Panyu Road

Radisson Plaza Xingguo Hotel

Huashan Road

Xingguo Road (Xingguo Lu)

(Hunan Lu)

Hunan Road

Ferguson Lane

GAO'AN ROAD
(SHANGHAI LIBRARY)

(Huaihai Zhonglu)

Shanghai Tushuguan
(Shanghai Library)

Guojie Jiaota
(Shanghai International Community Church)

Shama Luxe Huashan Apartments

Niuqiaobang

Xingfu Road (Xingfu Lu)

Huashan Road

Tai'an Road (Tai'an Lu)

Wukang Road

Iao Meiguo Xuesheng
(former Shanghai American School)

Gao Road

HENGSHAN ROAD
衡山路站

Wukang Lu

Yongjia Lu

Anting Road

(Wulumuqi

Wukang Dalou
(Normandie Apartments)

Kangping Lu

Yongjia Road

Anting Villa Hotel

Fahuazhen Road (Fahuazhen Lu)

Central Huaihai Road

Song Qingling
(Soong Ching Ling's former residence)

Wanping Rd

Regal International East Asia

Hengshan Lu

Jianguo Rd West

1

Shanghai Ying Cheng
(Shanghai Film Art Centre)

Xinhua Road (Xinhua Lu)

Panyu Rd

Hualhai Road West (Hualhai Xilu)

Huashan Road

Tianping Road

Viqing Road

Kangping Road

Zhongguo Gongchandang Shanghai Shi Wei Yuanhui
(Communist Party HQ)

HENGSHAN GONGYUAN

Zhongguo Tielu Gongren Jinian Ta
(Chinese Railroad Workers)

Hengshan Picardie Hotel

Wuxing Lu

Zhaojiabang Road

DONGAN ROA

Jiaotong Daxue
(Shanghai Jiaotong University)

Guangyuan Road

(Nanping Lu)

Hengshan Road

Xiao Hong Lou
(La Villa Rouge)

XUJIAHUI GONGYUAN

Zhaojiabang Road

Shanghai Mec
University

0 —— 500 m
0 —— 500 yds

A · B

136

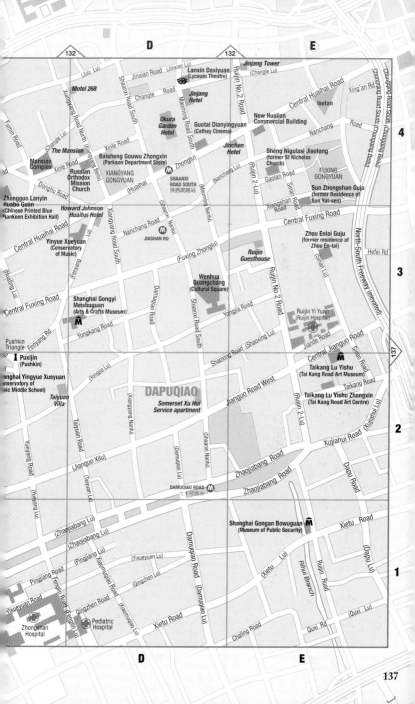

Motel 268

Jinjang Tower
(Changle Lu)

Lanxin Daxiyuan
(Lyceum Theatre)

Jinxian Road (Jinxian Lu)

Changle Road

Jinjang
Hotel

Maoming Road South

Ruijin No.2 Road

Central Huaihai Road

Xing'an Rd

Isetan

Chongqing Road South (Chongqing Beilu)

Chongqing Road South (Chongqing Beilu)

Okura
Garden
Hotel

Guotai Dianyingyuan
(Cathay Cinema)

New Hualian
Commercial Building

Nanchang
Road

Xinle Road

The Mansion

Jinchen
Hotel

Sheng Nigulasi Jiaotang
(former St Nicholas
Church)

FUXING
GONGYUAN

Mansion
Complex

Xinle Road

Baisheng Gouwu Zhongxin
(Parkson Department Store)

Zhonglu

Ruijin Lu

Gaolan Road

Farmn Road

Xiangyang Road North (Xiangyang Beilu)

Russian
Orthodox
Mission
Church

XIANGYANG
GONGYUAN

SHAANXI
ROAD SOUTH
陕西南路站

Maoming Road South

Nanchang Lu

Sinan Road

Sun Zhongshan Guju
(former Residence of
Sun Yat-sen)

Donghu Road

(Huaihai)

Xiangshan
Road

Zhongguo Lanyin
Huabu Guan
(Chinese Printed Blue
Nankeen Exhibition Hall)

Howard Johnson
Huaihai Hotel

Central Huaihai Road

(Shaanxi Namlu)

Central Fuxing Road

Zhou Enlai Guju
(former residence of
Zhou En-lai)

Nanchang Road South

Sinan Lu

North-South Freeway (elevated)

Hefei Rd

137

Yinyue Xueyuan
(Conservatory
of Music)

Fenyang

Xiangyang Road South

JIASHAN RD

(Fuxing Zhonglu)

Ruijin No.2 Road

(Haitang Lu)

Ruijin
Guesthouse

Central Fuxing Road

Damuqiao Road

Wenhua
Guangchang
(Cultural Square)

Yongjia Road

Ruijin Yi Yuan
(Ruijin Hospital)

Jiande Road

Shanghai Gongyi
Meishuguan
(Arts & Crafts Museum)

Yongkang Road

Shaanxi Road South

Yongjia Road (Yongjia Namlu)

Shaoxing Road (Shaoxing Lu)

Central Jianguo Road

Sinan Road

Pushkin
Triangle

Fenyang Rd

Central Jianguo Road

Taikang Lu Yishu
(Tai Kang Road Art Museum)

Puxijin
(Pushkin)

anghai Yingyue Xueyuan
onservatory of
sic Middle School)

Taikang Road

Taiyuan
Villa

DAPUQIAO

Somerset Xu Hui
Service apartment

Taikang Lu Yishu Zhongxin
(Tai Kang Road Art Centre)

Xiangyang Namlu

Ruijin 2-Lu

Kuaihuo Lu

Yueyang Road

Taiyuan Road

Jianguo Road West

Xujiahui Road

Dapu Road

Yueyang Lu

Taiyuan Road

(Jianguo Xilu)

Shaanxi Namlu

Damuqiao Road

Zhaojiabang Road

Zhaojiabang Road

DAMUQIAO ROAD
大木桥路

Pingjiang Road

(Zhaojiabang Lu)

(Zhaojiabang Lu)

Shanghai Gongan Bowuguan
(Museum of Public Security)

Xietu Road

Ruijin Road

Fenglin Road (Fenglin Lu)

Xiaomuqiao Road (Xiaomuqiao Lu)

(Yixueyuan Lu)

Xietu Lu

Rihui Branch

Pingjiang Road

Qingzhen Road

Damuqiao Road (Damuqiao Lu)

Yixueyuan Road

Zhongshan
Hospital

Qingzhen Road

Pediatric
Hospital

Xietu Road

Chaling Road

Quxi Rd

(Quxi Lu)

Dapu Lu

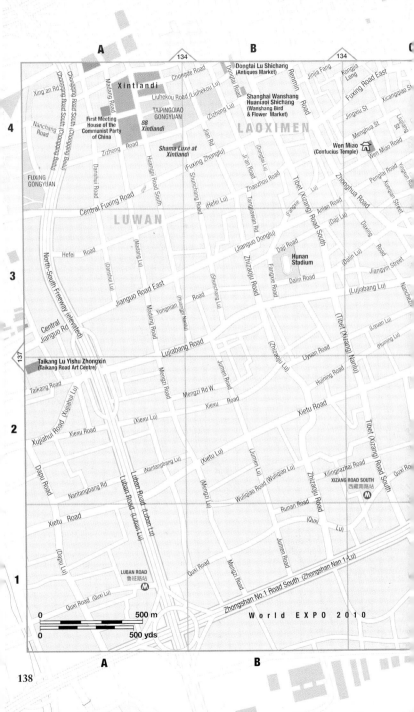

Chongqing Road South (Chongqing Nanlu)
Changle Road (Chongqing Beilu)

Xing'an Rd

Madang Road

Xintiandi

Chongde Road

Liuhekou Road (Liuhekou)

Zizhong Lu

Jinjia Fang

Kongjia
Long

Fuxing Road East

Xicangqiao St

Dongtai Lu Shichang
(Antiques Market)

Renmin Road

Jingxiu St

Xicangqiao St

Lijiang St

Menghua St

**Shanghai Wanshang
Huaniaoi Shichang**
(Wanshang Bird
& Flower Market)

Nanchang Road

**First Meeting
House of the
Communist Party
of China**

TAIPINGQIAO
GONGYUAN

**88
Xintiandi**

Jian Rd

LAOXIMEN

Wen Miao
(Confucius Temple)

Wen Miao Road

**Shama Luxe at
Xintiandi**

Danshui Road

Zizhong Road

Huangpi Road South

(Fuxing Zhonglu)

Shunchang Road

(Hefei Lu)

Jian Road

Dongtai Lu

Zhaozhou Road

Tanglawan Rd

Tibet (Xizang) Road South

Fangxie
Lu

Anran Road

Zhonghua Road

Penglai Road

Xuexian Street

Yingxun Rd

**FUXING
GONGYUAN**

Central Fuxing Road

LUWAN

(Jianguo Donglu)

Daji Road

(Daji Lu)

Daxing
Road

(Dalin Lu)

Hefei   Road

Madang Lu

(Danshui Lu)

Zhizaoju Road

**Hunan
Stadium**

Fangxie Road

Jiangyin Street

Nanche

North-South Freeway (elevated)

Jianguo Road East

Madang Road

Yongnian Road

(Huangpi Nanlu)

(Shunchang Lu)

Dalin Road

(Lujiabang Lu)

(Liyuan Lu)

Huining Lu

Central
Jianguo Rd

Lujiabang Road

(Zhizaoju Lu)

Lhuan Road

Lhuan Road

Taikang Lu Yishu Zhongxin
(Taikang Road Art Centre)

Mengzi Road

Jumen Road

Huining Road

Taikang Road

Mengzi Rd W.

Xiexu   Road

Xietu Road

Xujiahui Road (Xujiahui Lu)

Xiexu Road

(Xiexu Lu)

(Xietu Lu)

Jumen Lu

Xilingjiazhai Road

XIZANG ROAD SOUTH
西藏南路站

Tibet (Xizang) Road South

Quxi Rd

Dapu Road

Nantangbang Rd

(Nantangbang Lu)

Wuliqiao Road (Wuliqiao Lu)

Zhizaoju Road

(Mengzi Lu)

Xietu   Road

Runan Road

(Quxi

Lu)

(Dapu Lu)

Luban Road (Luban Lu)

Luban Road (Luban Lu)

Quxi Road

Mengzi Road

Jumen Road

Zhongshan No.1 Road South (Zhongshan Nan 1-Lu)

LUBAN ROAD
鲁班路站

Quxi Road (Quxi Lu)

World EXPO 2010

0   500 m

0   500 yds

Fuxing Rd East
(Fuxing Donglu)

Wangyun Road
Guangqi Road South (Guangqi Nanlu)
Lingji St
Laoxin St
Doushi Street
Waima Road

Penglai Rd
Penglai Rd
Miezhu Lu

Penglai Lu
Ninghe Road
Meijia St
Xundao Street (Xundao Jie)
Mejia St

Qiaojia Road
Zhonghua Road (Zhonghua Lu)
Zixia Road
Maojia Road

Road South
Yujia Long
Wangjiazuijiao Street
Beishijia St
Xinmatou Street

Shangwen Road
Huangjia Road
Wangjiamatou Road
Miezhu
Lu
Long
Zhuhangmatou St
Zhongshan Road South (Zhongshan Nanlu)
St

(Zhonghua Lu)
Maicang giao St
DONGJIADU
(Wangjiamatou Lu)
Wanyumatou St

(Henan Nanlu)
(Jiangyin Jie)
Dongjiadu Road (Dongjiadu Lu)
Xigouyu Road
Nangu St
Gongyimatou St

Sanyuan Street
Dongjiangyin Street
Laiyimatou Rd
Dongjiadu Tianzhutang (Dongjiadu Cathedral)
Waima St

Lujiabang Road
Liushi Road
Nancang Street
(Dongjiangyin Jie)
Luxi Street
Huiguan
St

Rd
(Huining Lu)
Hainan Long W.
Duojia Road
Nanlu)

Tianzhushan Rd
East
Haichao Road
Caonexan Road
Lujiabang Rd
(Duojia Lu)

Puyu Road West
South Bund Fabric Market
Youchematou St

Xietu Road East (Xietu Donglu)
Puyu
NANPU BRIDGE 南浦大桥站 Ⓜ
Nanliang St
(Waima St)

Chezhan Road East
Chezhan Rd West
Puyu (Quyu Lu)

Huangpu

Minjian Shoucangpin Chenlieguan/ Sanshan Huiguan (Museum of Folk Art)
PENGLAI GONGYUAN Ⓜ

Zhongshan Road South (Zhongshan Nanlu)
Nanpu Bridge (Nanpu Qiao)

W o r l d   E X P O   2 0 1 0

Tangnan Road
Nanmatou Road East
Jiaonan Road

W o r l d   E X P O   2 0 1 0
Sanliqiao Road East

World Expo Museum Ⓜ
W o r l d   E X P O   2 0 1 0

Yinan Road (Yinan Lu)
(Nanmatou Lu)
Pudong Road South
Pusan Rd

p132	p133		p140
		p134	p135
p136	p137	p138	p139

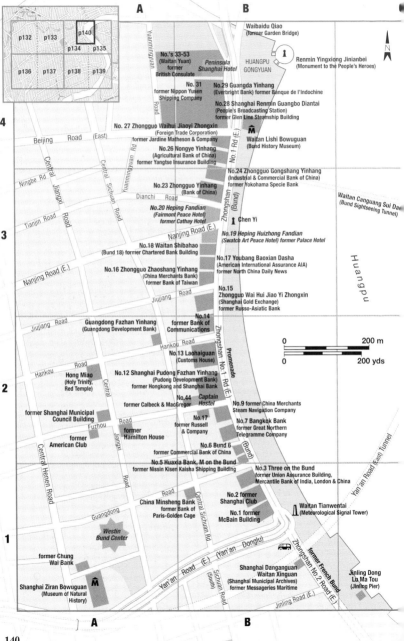

A   B

p132 | p133
p134 | p135
p140
p136 | p137 | p138 | p139

Waibaidu Qiao
(former Garden Bridge)

HUANGPU
GONGYUAN

Renmin Yingxiong Jinianbei
(Monument to the People's Heroes)

No.'s 33-53
(Waitan Yuan)
former
British Consulate

Peninsula
Shanghai Hotel

No. 31
former Nippon Yusen
Shipping Company

No.29 Guangda Yinhang
(Everbright Bank) former Banque de l'Indochine

No.28 Shanghai Renmin Guangbo Diantai
(People's Broadcasting Station)
former Glen Line Steamship Building

No. 27 Zhongguo Waihui Jiaoyi Zhongxin
(Foreign Trade Corporation)
former Jardine Matheson & Company

Waitan Lishi Bowuguan
(Bund History Museum)

No.26 Nongye Yinhang
(Agricultural Bank of China)
former Yangtse Insurance Building

No.24 Zhongguo Gongshang Yinhang
(Industrial & Commercial Bank of China)
former Yokohama Specie Bank

No.23 Zhongguo Yinhang
(Bank of China)

Waitan Canguang Sui Dao
(Bund Sightseeing Tunnel)

Dianchi   Road

No.20 Heping Fandian
(Fairmont Peace Hotel)
former Cathay Hotel

Chen Yi

Nanjing Road (E.)

No.19 Heping Huizhong Fandian
(Swatch Art Peace Hotel) former Palace Hotel

No.18 Waitan Shibahao
(Bund 18) former Chartered Bank Building

No.17 Youbang Baoxian Dasha
(American International Assurance AIA)
former North China Daily News

No.16 Zhongguo Zhaoshang Yinhang
(China Merchants Bank)
former Bank of Taiwan

No.15
Zhongguo Wai Hui Jiao Yi Zhongxin
(Shanghai Gold Exchange)
former Russo-Asiatic Bank

Jiujiang   Road

No.14
former Bank of
Communications

Huangpu

Guangdong Fazhan Yinhang
(Guangdong Development Bank)

Jiujiang   Road

Hankou   Road

No.13 Laohaiguan
(Customs House)

Hong Miao
(Holy Trinity,
Red Temple)

No.12 Shanghai Pudong Fazhan Yinhang
(Pudong Development Bank)
former Hongkong and Shanghai Bank

Hankou   Road

No.44   Captain
Hostel
former Calbeck & MacGregor

No.9 former China Merchants
Steam Navigation Company

former Shanghai Municipal
Council Building

No.17
former Russell
& Company

No.7 Bangkok Bank
former Great Northern
Telegramme Company

Fuzhou   Road

former
Hamilton House

former
American Club

No.6 Bund 6
former Commercial Bank of China

No.5 Huaxia Bank, M on the Bund
former Nissin Kisen Kaisha Shipping Building

No.3 Three on the Bund
former Union Assurance Building,
Mercantile Bank of India, London & China

Guangdong   Road

China Minsheng Bank
former Bank of
Paris-Golden Cage

No.2 former
Shanghai Club

No.1 former
McBain Building

Waitan Tianwentai
(Meteorological Signal Tower)

Westin
Bund Center

former Chung
Wai Bank

Yan'an Road Tunnel

former French Bund

former Chung
Wai Bank

Shanghai Dangancuan
Waitan Xinguan
(Shanghai Municipal Archives)
former Messageries Maritime

Jinling Dong
Lu Ma Tou
(Jinling Pier)

Shanghai Ziran Bowuguan
(Museum of Natural
History)

Yan'an   Road   (E.)   (Yan'an   Donglu)

Jinling   Road   (E.)

0   200 m

0   200 yds

Beijing   Road   (East)

Ningbo Rd.

Tianjin Road

Nanjing Road (E.)

Central   Jiangxi   Road

Central   Sichuan   Road

Yuanmingyuan   Rd.

Yuanmingyuan   Road

Zhongshan (Bund)

Zhongshan   No.1   Rd (E.)

No.1 Rd (E.)

Promenade

Central   Henen   Road

Central   Jiangxi   Road

Central   Sichuan   Rd.

Sichuan   Road   (South)

Zhongshan   No.2   Road (E.)

Atlas Index

PLACES OF INTEREST

HOTELS

PARKS

Index

Restaurants

Insight Smart Guide: Shanghai
Written by: **Brent Hannon**
Proofread and indexed by: **Neil Titman**
Photography by: **APA Ryan Pyle** except:
APA David Shen Kai, 2B, 3ML/MR, 4T, 5,
7B, 11B/T, 12, 17T/B, 19B, 23B/T, 25T,
26/27, 28/29, 30, 34, 39T, 47, 52/53,
60, 65T, 73, 78, 86, 88/89, 91,
100/101, 111, 126/127, 126, 128, **Curt**
110, Crowne Plaza 74, **Fairmont Peace**
Hotel, 34/35, **Fotolia** 62, **Four Seasons**
71, **Getty** 60/61, 61, 120, **Intercontinen-**
tal 76, **Istockphoto** 63, 64B, 65B, **Le**
Royal Meridian 40T, 68/69, **Livepine**
109T, **Peninsula Hotel** 38M, **Raddisson**
Hotels 38B, 89, 103, **St Regis** 77, **Swis-**
sotel 72, **marc Van der Chrijs** 109B,
West Bund Centre 69, 92, **Roger Wo** 44
Picture Manager: **Steven Lawrence**
Maps: **Stephen Ramsay**

Series Editor: **Jason Mitchell**
First Edition 2010
© 2010 Apa Publications GmbH & Co.
Verlag KG Singapore Branch, Singapore.
Printed in Singapore by Insight Print
Services (Pte) Ltd
Worldwide distribution enquiries:
Apa Publications GmbH & Co. Verlag KG
(Singapore Branch) 38 Joo Koon Road, Sin-
gapore 628990; tel: (65) 6865 1600; fax:
(65) 6861 6438
Distributed in the UK and Ireland by:
GeoCenter International Ltd
Meridian House, Churchill Way West, Bas-
ingstoke, Hampshire RG21 6YR;tel: (44
1256) 817 987; fax: (44 1256) 817 988
Distributed in the United States by:
Langenscheidt Publishers, Inc.
36–36 33rd Street 4th Floor, Long Island
City, New York 11106; tel: (1 718) 784

0055; fax: (1 718) 784 0640l
Contacting the Editors
We would appreciate it if readers would alert
us to errors or outdated information by writ-
ing to:
Apa Publications, PO Box 7910, London SE1
1WE, UK; fax: (44 20) 7403 0290;
e-mail: insight@apaguide.co.uk
No part of this book may be reproduced,
stored in a retrieval system or transmitted in
any form or by any means (electronic,
mechanical, photocopying, recording or other-
wise), without prior written permission of Apa
Publications. Brief text quotations with use of
photographs are exempted for book review
purposes only. Information has been obtained
from sources believed to be reliable, but its
accuracy and completeness, and the opinions
based thereon, are not guaranteed.